MTTC
Spanish (028) Test

SECRETS

Study Guide
Your Key to Exam Success

MTTC Exam Review for the
Michigan Test for Teacher Certification

Dear Future Exam Success Story:

First of all, **THANK YOU** for purchasing Mometrix study materials!

Second, congratulations! You are one of the few determined test-takers who are committed to doing whatever it takes to excel on your exam. **You have come to the right place.** We developed these study materials with one goal in mind: to deliver you the information you need in a format that's concise and easy to use.

In addition to optimizing your guide for the content of the test, we've outlined our recommended steps for breaking down the preparation process into small, attainable goals so you can make sure you stay on track.

We've also analyzed the entire test-taking process, identifying the most common pitfalls and showing how you can overcome them and be ready for any curveball the test throws you.

Standardized testing is one of the biggest obstacles on your road to success, which only increases the importance of doing well in the high-pressure, high-stakes environment of test day. Your results on this test could have a significant impact on your future, and this guide provides the information and practical advice to help you achieve your full potential on test day.

Your success is our success

We would love to hear from you! If you would like to share the story of your exam success or if you have any questions or comments in regard to our products, please contact us at **800-673-8175** or **support@mometrix.com**.

Thanks again for your business and we wish you continued success!

Sincerely,
The Mometrix Test Preparation Team

Need more help? Check out our flashcards at: http://mometrixflashcards.com/MTTC

TABLE OF CONTENTS

Introduction

Thank you for purchasing this resource! You have made the choice to prepare yourself for a test that could have a huge impact on your future, and this guide is designed to help you be fully ready for test day. Obviously, it's important to have a solid understanding of the test material, but you also need to be prepared for the unique environment and stressors of the test, so that you can perform to the best of your abilities.

For this purpose, the first section that appears in this guide is the **Secret Keys**. We've devoted countless hours to meticulously researching what works and what doesn't, and we've boiled down our findings to the five most impactful steps you can take to improve your performance on the test. We start at the beginning with study planning and move through the preparation process, all the way to the testing strategies that will help you get the most out of what you know when you're finally sitting in front of the test.

We recommend that you start preparing for your test as far in advance as possible. However, if you've bought this guide as a last-minute study resource and only have a few days before your test, we recommend that you skip over the first two Secret Keys since they address a long-term study plan.

If you struggle with **test anxiety**, we strongly encourage you to check out our recommendations for how you can overcome it. Test anxiety is a formidable foe, but it can be beaten, and we want to make sure you have the tools you need to defeat it.

Secret Key #1 – Plan Big, Study Small

There's a lot riding on your performance. If you want to ace this test, you're going to need to keep your skills sharp and the material fresh in your mind. You need a plan that lets you review everything you need to know while still fitting in your schedule. We'll break this strategy down into three categories.

Information Organization

Start with the information you already have: the official test outline. From this, you can make a complete list of all the concepts you need to cover before the test. Organize these concepts into groups that can be studied together, and create a list of any related vocabulary you need to learn so you can brush up on any difficult terms. You'll want to keep this vocabulary list handy once you actually start studying since you may need to add to it along the way.

Time Management

Once you have your set of study concepts, decide how to spread them out over the time you have left before the test. Break your study plan into small, clear goals so you have a manageable task for each day and know exactly what you're doing. Then just focus on one small step at a time. When you manage your time this way, you don't need to spend hours at a time studying. Studying a small block of content for a short period each day helps you retain information better and avoid stressing over how much you have left to do. You can relax knowing that you have a plan to cover everything in time. In order for this strategy to be effective though, you have to start studying early and stick to your schedule. Avoid the exhaustion and futility that comes from last-minute cramming!

Study Environment

The environment you study in has a big impact on your learning. Studying in a coffee shop, while probably more enjoyable, is not likely to be as fruitful as studying in a quiet room. It's important to keep distractions to a minimum. You're only planning to study for a short block of time, so make the most of it. Don't pause to check your phone or get up to find a snack. It's also important to **avoid multitasking**. Research has consistently shown that multitasking will make your studying dramatically less effective. Your study area should also be comfortable and well-lit so you don't have the distraction of straining your eyes or sitting on an uncomfortable chair.

The time of day you study is also important. You want to be rested and alert. Don't wait until just before bedtime. Study when you'll be most likely to comprehend and remember. Even better, if you know what time of day your test will be, set that time aside for study. That way your brain will be used to working on that subject at that specific time and you'll have a better chance of recalling information.

Finally, it can be helpful to team up with others who are studying for the same test. Your actual studying should be done in as isolated an environment as possible, but the work of organizing the information and setting up the study plan can be divided up. In between study sessions, you can discuss with your teammates the concepts that you're all studying and quiz each other on the details. Just be sure that your teammates are as serious about the test as you are. If you find that your study time is being replaced with social time, you might need to find a new team.

Secret Key #2 – Make Your Studying Count

You're devoting a lot of time and effort to preparing for this test, so you want to be absolutely certain it will pay off. This means doing more than just reading the content and hoping you can remember it on test day. It's important to make every minute of study count. There are two main areas you can focus on to make your studying count:

Retention

It doesn't matter how much time you study if you can't remember the material. You need to make sure you are retaining the concepts. To check your retention of the information you're learning, try recalling it at later times with minimal prompting. Try carrying around flashcards and glance at one or two from time to time or ask a friend who's also studying for the test to quiz you.

To enhance your retention, look for ways to put the information into practice so that you can apply it rather than simply recalling it. If you're using the information in practical ways, it will be much easier to remember. Similarly, it helps to solidify a concept in your mind if you're not only reading it to yourself but also explaining it to someone else. Ask a friend to let you teach them about a concept you're a little shaky on (or speak aloud to an imaginary audience if necessary). As you try to summarize, define, give examples, and answer your friend's questions, you'll understand the concepts better and they will stay with you longer. Finally, step back for a big picture view and ask yourself how each piece of information fits with the whole subject. When you link the different concepts together and see them working together as a whole, it's easier to remember the individual components.

Finally, practice showing your work on any multi-step problems, even if you're just studying. Writing out each step you take to solve a problem will help solidify the process in your mind, and you'll be more likely to remember it during the test.

Modality

Modality simply refers to the means or method by which you study. Choosing a study modality that fits your own individual learning style is crucial. No two people learn best in exactly the same way, so it's important to know your strengths and use them to your advantage.

For example, if you learn best by visualization, focus on visualizing a concept in your mind and draw an image or a diagram. Try color-coding your notes, illustrating them, or creating symbols that will trigger your mind to recall a learned concept. If you learn best by hearing or discussing information, find a study partner who learns the same way or read aloud to yourself. Think about how to put the information in your own words. Imagine that you are giving a lecture on the topic and record yourself so you can listen to it later.

For any learning style, flashcards can be helpful. Organize the information so you can take advantage of spare moments to review. Underline key words or phrases. Use different colors for different categories. Mnemonic devices (such as creating a short list in which every item starts with the same letter) can also help with retention. Find what works best for you and use it to store the information in your mind most effectively and easily.

Secret Key #3 – Practice the Right Way

Your success on test day depends not only on how many hours you put into preparing, but also on whether you prepared the right way. It's good to check along the way to see if your studying is paying off. One of the most effective ways to do this is by taking practice tests to evaluate your progress. Practice tests are useful because they show exactly where you need to improve. Every time you take a practice test, pay special attention to these three groups of questions:

- The questions you got wrong
- The questions you had to guess on, even if you guessed right
- The questions you found difficult or slow to work through

This will show you exactly what your weak areas are, and where you need to devote more study time. Ask yourself why each of these questions gave you trouble. Was it because you didn't understand the material? Was it because you didn't remember the vocabulary? Do you need more repetitions on this type of question to build speed and confidence? Dig into those questions and figure out how you can strengthen your weak areas as you go back to review the material.

Additionally, many practice tests have a section explaining the answer choices. It can be tempting to read the explanation and think that you now have a good understanding of the concept. However, an explanation likely only covers part of the question's broader context. Even if the explanation makes sense, **go back and investigate** every concept related to the question until you're positive you have a thorough understanding.

As you go along, keep in mind that the practice test is just that: practice. Memorizing these questions and answers will not be very helpful on the actual test because it is unlikely to have any of the same exact questions. If you only know the right answers to the sample questions, you won't be prepared for the real thing. **Study the concepts** until you understand them fully, and then you'll be able to answer any question that shows up on the test.

It's important to wait on the practice tests until you're ready. If you take a test on your first day of study, you may be overwhelmed by the amount of material covered and how much you need to learn. Work up to it gradually.

On test day, you'll need to be prepared for answering questions, managing your time, and using the test-taking strategies you've learned. It's a lot to balance, like a mental marathon that will have a big impact on your future. Like training for a marathon, you'll need to start slowly and work your way up. When test day arrives, you'll be ready.

Start with the strategies you've read in the first two Secret Keys—plan your course and study in the way that works best for you. If you have time, consider using multiple study resources to get different approaches to the same concepts. It can be helpful to see difficult concepts from more than one angle. Then find a good source for practice tests. Many times, the test website will suggest potential study resources or provide sample tests.

Practice Test Strategy

When you're ready to start taking practice tests, follow this strategy:

Untimed and Open-Book Practice

Take the first test with no time constraints and with your notes and study guide handy. Take your time and focus on applying the strategies you've learned.

Timed and Open-Book Practice

Take the second practice test open-book as well, but set a timer and practice pacing yourself to finish in time.

Timed and Closed-Book Practice

Take any other practice tests as if it were test day. Set a timer and put away your study materials. Sit at a table or desk in a quiet room, imagine yourself at the testing center, and answer questions as quickly and accurately as possible.

Keep repeating timed and closed-book tests on a regular basis until you run out of practice tests or it's time for the actual test. Your mind will be ready for the schedule and stress of test day, and you'll be able to focus on recalling the material you've learned.

Secret Key #4 – Pace Yourself

Once you're fully prepared for the material on the test, your biggest challenge on test day will be managing your time. Just knowing that the clock is ticking can make you panic even if you have plenty of time left. Work on pacing yourself so you can build confidence against the time constraints of the exam. Pacing is a difficult skill to master, especially in a high-pressure environment, so **practice is vital**.

Set time expectations for your pace based on how much time is available. For example, if a section has 60 questions and the time limit is 30 minutes, you know you have to average 30 seconds or less per question in order to answer them all. Although 30 seconds is the hard limit, set 25 seconds per question as your goal, so you reserve extra time to spend on harder questions. When you budget extra time for the harder questions, you no longer have any reason to stress when those questions take longer to answer.

Don't let this time expectation distract you from working through the test at a calm, steady pace, but keep it in mind so you don't spend too much time on any one question. Recognize that taking extra time on one question you don't understand may keep you from answering two that you do understand later in the test. If your time limit for a question is up and you're still not sure of the answer, mark it and move on, and come back to it later if the time and the test format allow. If the testing format doesn't allow you to return to earlier questions, just make an educated guess; then put it out of your mind and move on.

On the easier questions, be careful not to rush. It may seem wise to hurry through them so you have more time for the challenging ones, but it's not worth missing one if you know the concept and just didn't take the time to read the question fully. Work efficiently but make sure you understand the question and have looked at all of the answer choices, since more than one may seem right at first.

Even if you're paying attention to the time, you may find yourself a little behind at some point. You should speed up to get back on track, but do so wisely. Don't panic; just take a few seconds less on each question until you're caught up. Don't guess without thinking, but do look through the answer choices and eliminate any you know are wrong. If you can get down to two choices, it is often worthwhile to guess from those. Once you've chosen an answer, move on and don't dwell on any that you skipped or had to hurry through. If a question was taking too long, chances are it was one of the harder ones, so you weren't as likely to get it right anyway.

On the other hand, if you find yourself getting ahead of schedule, it may be beneficial to slow down a little. The more quickly you work, the more likely you are to make a careless mistake that will affect your score. You've budgeted time for each question, so don't be afraid to spend that time. Practice an efficient but careful pace to get the most out of the time you have.

Secret Key #5 – Have a Plan for Guessing

When you're taking the test, you may find yourself stuck on a question. Some of the answer choices seem better than others, but you don't see the one answer choice that is obviously correct. What do you do?

The scenario described above is very common, yet most test takers have not effectively prepared for it. Developing and practicing a plan for guessing may be one of the single most effective uses of your time as you get ready for the exam.

In developing your plan for guessing, there are three questions to address:

- When should you start the guessing process?
- How should you narrow down the choices?
- Which answer should you choose?

When to Start the Guessing Process

Unless your plan for guessing is to select C every time (which, despite its merits, is not what we recommend), you need to leave yourself enough time to apply your answer elimination strategies. Since you have a limited amount of time for each question, that means that if you're going to give yourself the best shot at guessing correctly, you have to decide quickly whether or not you will guess.

Of course, the best-case scenario is that you don't have to guess at all, so first, see if you can answer the question based on your knowledge of the subject and basic reasoning skills. Focus on the key words in the question and try to jog your memory of related topics. Give yourself a chance to bring the knowledge to mind, but once you realize that you don't have (or you can't access) the knowledge you need to answer the question, it's time to start the guessing process.

It's almost always better to start the guessing process too early than too late. It only takes a few seconds to remember something and answer the question from knowledge. Carefully eliminating wrong answer choices takes longer. Plus, going through the process of eliminating answer choices can actually help jog your memory.

Summary: Start the guessing process as soon as you decide that you can't answer the question based on your knowledge.

How to Narrow Down the Choices

The next chapter in this book (**Test-Taking Strategies**) includes a wide range of strategies for how to approach questions and how to look for answer choices to eliminate. You will definitely want to read those carefully, practice them, and figure out which ones work best for you. Here though, we're going to address a mindset rather than a particular strategy.

Your chances of guessing an answer correctly depend on how many options you are choosing from.

How many choices you have	How likely you are to guess correctly
5	20%
4	25%
3	33%
2	50%
1	100%

You can see from this chart just how valuable it is to be able to eliminate incorrect answers and make an educated guess, but there are two things that many test takers do that cause them to miss out on the benefits of guessing:

- Accidentally eliminating the correct answer
- Selecting an answer based on an impression

We'll look at the first one here, and the second one in the next section.

To avoid accidentally eliminating the correct answer, we recommend a thought exercise called **the $5 challenge**. In this challenge, you only eliminate an answer choice from contention if you are willing to bet $5 on it being wrong. Why $5? Five dollars is a small but not insignificant amount of money. It's an amount you could afford to lose but wouldn't want to throw away. And while losing $5 once might not hurt too much, doing it twenty times will set you back $100. In the same way, each small decision you make—eliminating a choice here, guessing on a question there—won't by itself impact your score very much, but when you put them all together, they can make a big difference. By holding each answer choice elimination decision to a higher standard, you can reduce the risk of accidentally eliminating the correct answer.

The $5 challenge can also be applied in a positive sense: If you are willing to bet $5 that an answer choice *is* correct, go ahead and mark it as correct.

Summary: Only eliminate an answer choice if you are willing to bet $5 that it is wrong.

Which Answer to Choose

You're taking the test. You've run into a hard question and decided you'll have to guess. You've eliminated all the answer choices you're willing to bet $5 on. Now you have to pick an answer. Why do we even need to talk about this? Why can't you just pick whichever one you feel like when the time comes?

The answer to these questions is that if you don't come into the test with a plan, you'll rely on your impression to select an answer choice, and if you do that, you risk falling into a trap. The test writers know that everyone who takes their test will be guessing on some of the questions, so they intentionally write wrong answer choices to seem plausible. You still have to pick an answer though, and if the wrong answer choices are designed to look right, how can you ever be sure that you're not falling for their trap? The best solution we've found to this dilemma is to take the decision out of your hands entirely. Here is the process we recommend:

Once you've eliminated any choices that you are confident (willing to bet $5) are wrong, select the first remaining choice as your answer.

Whether you choose to select the first remaining choice, the second, or the last, the important thing is that you use some preselected standard. Using this approach guarantees that you will not be enticed into selecting an answer choice that looks right, because you are not basing your decision on how the answer choices look.

This is not meant to make you question your knowledge. Instead, it is to help you recognize the difference between your knowledge and your impressions. There's a huge difference between thinking an answer is right because of what you know, and thinking an answer is right because it looks or sounds like it should be right.

Summary: To ensure that your selection is appropriately random, make a predetermined selection from among all answer choices you have not eliminated.

Test-Taking Strategies

This section contains a list of test-taking strategies that you may find helpful as you work through the test. By taking what you know and applying logical thought, you can maximize your chances of answering any question correctly!

It is very important to realize that every question is different and every person is different: no single strategy will work on every question, and no single strategy will work for every person. That's why we've included all of them here, so you can try them out and determine which ones work best for different types of questions and which ones work best for you.

Question Strategies

Read Carefully

Read the question and answer choices carefully. Don't miss the question because you misread the terms. You have plenty of time to read each question thoroughly and make sure you understand what is being asked. Yet a happy medium must be attained, so don't waste too much time. You must read carefully, but efficiently.

Contextual Clues

Look for contextual clues. If the question includes a word you are not familiar with, look at the immediate context for some indication of what the word might mean. Contextual clues can often give you all the information you need to decipher the meaning of an unfamiliar word. Even if you can't determine the meaning, you may be able to narrow down the possibilities enough to make a solid guess at the answer to the question.

Prefixes

If you're having trouble with a word in the question or answer choices, try dissecting it. Take advantage of every clue that the word might include. Prefixes and suffixes can be a huge help. Usually they allow you to determine a basic meaning. Pre- means before, post- means after, pro - is positive, de- is negative. From prefixes and suffixes, you can get an idea of the general meaning of the word and try to put it into context.

Hedge Words

Watch out for critical hedge words, such as *likely, may, can, sometimes, often, almost, mostly, usually, generally, rarely*, and *sometimes*. Question writers insert these hedge phrases to cover every possibility. Often an answer choice will be wrong simply because it leaves no room for exception. Be on guard for answer choices that have definitive words such as *exactly* and *always*.

Switchback Words

Stay alert for *switchbacks*. These are the words and phrases frequently used to alert you to shifts in thought. The most common switchback words are *but, although*, and *however*. Others include *nevertheless, on the other hand, even though, while, in spite of, despite, regardless of*. Switchback words are important to catch because they can change the direction of the question or an answer choice.

Face Value

When in doubt, use common sense. Accept the situation in the problem at face value. Don't read too much into it. These problems will not require you to make wild assumptions. If you have to go beyond creativity and warp time or space in order to have an answer choice fit the question, then you should move on and consider the other answer choices. These are normal problems rooted in reality. The applicable relationship or explanation may not be readily apparent, but it is there for you to figure out. Use your common sense to interpret anything that isn't clear.

Answer Choice Strategies

Answer Selection

The most thorough way to pick an answer choice is to identify and eliminate wrong answers until only one is left, then confirm it is the correct answer. Sometimes an answer choice may immediately seem right, but be careful. The test writers will usually put more than one reasonable answer choice on each question, so take a second to read all of them and make sure that the other choices are not equally obvious. As long as you have time left, it is better to read every answer choice than to pick the first one that looks right without checking the others.

Answer Choice Families

An answer choice family consists of two (in rare cases, three) answer choices that are very similar in construction and cannot all be true at the same time. If you see two answer choices that are direct opposites or parallels, one of them is usually the correct answer. For instance, if one answer choice says that quantity x increases and another either says that quantity x decreases (opposite) or says that quantity y increases (parallel), then those answer choices would fall into the same family. An answer choice that doesn't match the construction of the answer choice family is more likely to be incorrect. Most questions will not have answer choice families, but when they do appear, you should be prepared to recognize them.

Eliminate Answers

Eliminate answer choices as soon as you realize they are wrong, but make sure you consider all possibilities. If you are eliminating answer choices and realize that the last one you are left with is also wrong, don't panic. Start over and consider each choice again. There may be something you missed the first time that you will realize on the second pass.

Avoid Fact Traps

Don't be distracted by an answer choice that is factually true but doesn't answer the question. You are looking for the choice that answers the question. Stay focused on what the question is asking for so you don't accidentally pick an answer that is true but incorrect. Always go back to the question and make sure the answer choice you've selected actually answers the question and is not merely a true statement.

Extreme Statements

In general, you should avoid answers that put forth extreme actions as standard practice or proclaim controversial ideas as established fact. An answer choice that states the "process should be used in certain situations, if..." is much more likely to be correct than one that states the "process should be discontinued completely." The first is a calm rational statement and doesn't even make a

- 11 -

definitive, uncompromising stance, using a hedge word *if* to provide wiggle room, whereas the second choice is a radical idea and far more extreme.

Benchmark

As you read through the answer choices and you come across one that seems to answer the question well, mentally select that answer choice. This is not your final answer, but it's the one that will help you evaluate the other answer choices. The one that you selected is your benchmark or standard for judging each of the other answer choices. Every other answer choice must be compared to your benchmark. That choice is correct until proven otherwise by another answer choice beating it. If you find a better answer, then that one becomes your new benchmark. Once you've decided that no other choice answers the question as well as your benchmark, you have your final answer.

Predict the Answer

Before you even start looking at the answer choices, it is often best to try to predict the answer. When you come up with the answer on your own, it is easier to avoid distractions and traps because you will know exactly what to look for. The right answer choice is unlikely to be word-for-word what you came up with, but it should be a close match. Even if you are confident that you have the right answer, you should still take the time to read each option before moving on.

General Strategies

Tough Questions

If you are stumped on a problem or it appears too hard or too difficult, don't waste time. Move on! Remember though, if you can quickly check for obviously incorrect answer choices, your chances of guessing correctly are greatly improved. Before you completely give up, at least try to knock out a couple of possible answers. Eliminate what you can and then guess at the remaining answer choices before moving on.

Check Your Work

Since you will probably not know every term listed and the answer to every question, it is important that you get credit for the ones that you do know. Don't miss any questions through careless mistakes. If at all possible, try to take a second to look back over your answer selection and make sure you've selected the correct answer choice and haven't made a costly careless mistake (such as marking an answer choice that you didn't mean to mark). This quick double check should more than pay for itself in caught mistakes for the time it costs.

Pace Yourself

It's easy to be overwhelmed when you're looking at a page full of questions; your mind is confused and full of random thoughts, and the clock is ticking down faster than you would like. Calm down and maintain the pace that you have set for yourself. Especially as you get down to the last few minutes of the test, don't let the small numbers on the clock make you panic. As long as you are on track by monitoring your pace, you are guaranteed to have time for each question.

Don't Rush

It is very easy to make errors when you are in a hurry. Maintaining a fast pace in answering questions is pointless if it makes you miss questions that you would have gotten right otherwise. Test writers like to include distracting information and wrong answers that seem right. Taking a little extra time to avoid careless mistakes can make all the difference in your test score. Find a pace that allows you to be confident in the answers that you select.

Keep Moving

Panicking will not help you pass the test, so do your best to stay calm and keep moving. Taking deep breaths and going through the answer elimination steps you practiced can help to break through a stress barrier and keep your pace.

Final Notes

The combination of a solid foundation of content knowledge and the confidence that comes from practicing your plan for applying that knowledge is the key to maximizing your performance on test day. As your foundation of content knowledge is built up and strengthened, you'll find that the strategies included in this chapter become more and more effective in helping you quickly sift through the distractions and traps of the test to isolate the correct answer.

Now it's time to move on to the test content chapters of this book, but be sure to keep your goal in mind. As you read, think about how you will be able to apply this information on the test. If you've already seen sample questions for the test and you have an idea of the question format and style, try to come up with questions of your own that you can answer based on what you're reading. This will give you valuable practice applying your knowledge in the same ways you can expect to on test day.

Good luck and good studying!

Language Structures and Comparisons

Phonetic language

Spanish is a purely phonetic language, which means that every letter, vowels as well as consonants, and combination of letters have their own associated sound. This associated sound is used every single time that this particular letter or combination of letters appears in a word. Therefore, as in all phonetic languages, if you know how to spell a word, you know how to pronounce it. The only exceptions are words adopted from foreign languages. Like in most other language, foreign or nonnative words are sometimes pronounced in Spanish the same way they are pronounced in the original language. In some cases, though, the original pronunciation is modified, and how and in which way it is modified varies by region.

Spanish pronunciation of vowels

Spanish has five vowels, the same as in English, but they are different from English in the sense they have one and only one associated sound regardless of their position in the word and which letters come before and after them. For example, the vowel *a* in Spanish is always pronounced like a shorter version of the *a* in car. There is no difference in the way it sounds whether it is at the beginning of the word (amanecer), between two consonants (caro), between a consonant and a vowel (caer, teatro) or at the end of the word (mesa). In English, though, the vowel *a* has multiple sounds and is pronounced differently in, for example, apple, daughter, day, walk, and also. The same rule applies to *e*, *i*, *o*, and *u*: there is only one sound for each of them.

Pronunciation of the letter *r* in Spanish

The letter *r* has two distinctively different pronunciations in Spanish: a soft one, similar to the English *tt* or *dd* sounds (as in jetty or Eddie), and a strong, rolling one. The soft sound is used whenever a single letter *r* is in the middle of a word between two vowels (caro, puro, aire), between a vowel and most consonants (tren, jardín, parte), and at the end of a word (caminar, comer, recibir). At the beginning of a word (reto, rápido, rojo) or after the consonants *l*, *n*, and *s* (alrededor, sonrisa, Israel), the single letter *r* is pronounced with the trilling sound used in the "double r" or *rr* phoneme.

Pronunciation of the "double r" in Spanish

The "double r" or *rr* is not considered a separate letter, but it is a very frequently used phoneme in Spanish. Some common words that include the *rr* are *correr*, *perro*, *arriba*, *carro*. The *rr* has a trilling sound that can be achieved by flapping the tongue against the front of the mouth. If properly rolled, the *rr* sound should be similar to the one you get when you try to imitate a motor. Be aware that the *rr* is used only between vowels. A similar trilling sound at the beginning of a word or after certain consonants (*l*, *n*, *s*) is spelled with a single *r*.

Regional differences in pronunciation of the "double l"

The way the "double l" sounds varies by region, and sometimes even within the same country. In most Spanish speaking areas, the *ll* has a soft sound similar to the English *y* in yes or yellow. In many parts of Argentina and Uruguay, however, the *ll* is much stronger and is pronounced like the *zh* phoneme found in English in words such as measure and pleasure. Common words that have the *ll* phoneme are lluvia (rain), llave (key), llorar (cry), and llegar (arrive).

Pronunciation of the letter *h* in Spanish and English

In English, the letter *h* has a soft, aspirated sound. In Spanish, by contrast, it is always completely silent. Most of the words that contain a letter *h* in Spanish have Latin or Greek roots, and the *h* has been kept just for etymological reasons. The only exceptions to this rule are some foreign words with no equivalent spelling in Spanish such as Hawaii, hamster, and hobby. In those cases, the letter *h* sounds like the Spanish letter *j*. When the letter *h* follows the letter *c* (mucho, chacra, chancho), it forms a new, different phoneme *ch* which has its own particular sound.

Pronunciations of the letter *g* in Spanish

When followed by a consonant (regla, negro) or by the vowels *a*, *o*, or *u* (gaviota, agosto, gusto), the sound of the letter *g* in Spanish is similar to the sound of that same letter in English words, such as good and game. If the letter *g* is followed by the vowels *e* and *i* (generar, registro), the sound of the letter *g* in Spanish is like the sound of the Spanish *j* (a very hard English *h*). If there is a *u* between the letter *g* and the vowels *e* or *i* (guerra, guiso), the letter *g* recovers its soft sound.

Existence of the letter *ñ* in Spanish

The letter *ñ* does not exist in English, and, although it is written as an *n* with a ~ on top, it is completely distinct from the letter *n*. In Spanish, it can be found in words such as mañana (morning or tomorrow), año (year), señor (mister), niña (girl), etc. The most similar sounds in English that resemble the *ñ* in Spanish are the *ny* or *ni* phonemes as found in words such as canyon, onion, or opinion, but pronounced fairly stronger. In the Spanish alphabet the *ñ* is located after the letter *n*.

Pronunciation of the letter *y* in Spanish

In Spanish, the letter *y* is treated as a vowel. At the end of a word (rey, muy, soy), it is always pronounce as the vowel *i*. If the letter *y* is before a vowel (yo, ya, yarda), in most countries it is also pronounced as the vowel *i*. However, in Argentina and Uruguay, the letter *y* before another vowel sounds more like the *sh* English phoneme as found in words such as shower and show.

Pronunciation of the letter *ch* in Spanish and English

The Spanish *ch* is different from English in the sense that it is always pronounced the same way. It has the exact same sound as found in English words such as church, charcoal, and march. Spanish dictionaries have a separate section for the *ch*, and it is located after the letter *c*. Common words in Spanish with *ch* are chancho, chispa, chino, chaqueta, etc.

Pronunciation of the "double c" in Spanish

Occidente, collección, and diccionario are some words in Spanish that use the "double c" or *cc*. In this phoneme, the first *c* has the strong sound of an English *k*, while the second *c* is much softer and has the same sound as an *s*. Overall, the *cc* sounds mostly like the same combination of letters sound in English in words such as accident and access, or like the *x* sound found in x-ray and excess.

Letter *w* in Spanish

The letter *w* is not native to the Spanish language, and it appears only in words that come from other languages. Depending on the country, it is called "uve doble," "v doble," "doble u," or "doble v." Words in Spanish with a *w* have mostly English roots (waterpolo, hawaiano, whisky) and are usually pronounced with the English *w* sound as found in water, when, winter, etc. In some countries, however, the *w* is pronounced with a very soft *g* added before the English *w* for a *gu* sound.

Pronunciation of the letter *j* in Spanish

The letter *j* has a completely different pronunciation from that of the same letter in English. Actually, the sound of the Spanish *j* does not exist in English. The closest sound would be an extremely hard and strong *h*, an exaggeration of the sound in words such as hot and home. In some regions, the *j* is pronounced slightly softer but it still is much harder than the English *h*. Be aware that in Spanish, the letter *g*, when followed by the vowels *e* as in género and digerir or *i* as in registrar and higiene, has the same strong sound as the letter *j*.

Pronunciations of the letter *c* in Spanish

The letter *c* has two different pronunciations depending on which letter is after it, much as it is in English. If followed by an *a* (camino), *o* (correr), *u* (cuñado), or a consonant (conectar), the letter *c* sounds like the English hard *c* in come and camera or the *k* in break and kimono. If followed by the vowels *e* (centro) or *i* (cigarillo), the letter *c* sounds like the *c* in face and celery. In some countries, Spain for example, the *s* sound of the letter *c* is much softer, almost like the sound of the letter *z*. Note that in the particular case of the letter *c* followed by the consonant *h* (chico), it forms the new letter *ch*, which has a similar sound as the English *ch* in church.

Spelling of the phoneme *f* in English and Spanish

The sound of the phoneme *f* in Spanish is the same as the sound of that phoneme in English as found in words such as family and future. It is never pronounced with the *v* sound found in *of* for example. Another major difference is that the phoneme *f* is obtained in Spanish only by the use of the letter *f*, while in English the same sound appears in words with *f* (face), *ff* (coffin), and *ph* (photograph). The letter *f* is never doubled and the *ph* combination does not exist in Spanish. In some foreign words the *ph* has been replaced by a single *f* (telephone–teléfono, photograph-fotografía).

Letter *q* in Spanish

In Spanish, the letter *q* has the sound of the English letter *k*. The letter *q* is always followed by a *u* (*qu*) and then either an *e* (querido, quebrar, quemar, quedar, quejido) or an *i* (quizá, quitar, quince, quirúrgico, quieto). There are very few exceptions (quantum, quorum) and they all have foreign roots.

Letter *z* in Spanish

In Spanish the letter *z*, regardless of which letter comes after it, has the same sound as the letter *c* before an *e* (centauro) or *i* (cocina). Therefore, in most of Latin America countries, it sounds like the *s* in English words such as silence and serious, while in most of Spain it sounds like the *th* in English words such as think and thunder. In Spanish, the letter *z* cannot be used before an *e* or *i* except in words of foreign origin (zepelin, zigzaguear). Due to this rule, the letter *z* is replaced by a *c* when forming the plural of words ending in *z* (lápiz/lápices, tapiz/tapices).

Rules for the written stress or accent mark

The Spanish language uses a written stress or accent mark on vowels to denote exceptions to its stressing rules. Words with a stress in the last syllable will have a written stress or accent mark if they end in a vowel (mamá, café, así) or the consonants *n* (camión, común, jamón) or *s* (jamás, francés, anís). For those words stressed in the second-to-last syllable, an accent mark is needed when they end in any consonant (ángel, álbum, cadáver, lápiz) except *n* and *s*. For words stressed in the third-to-last syllable, a written stress is always required, regardless of the last letter (apéndice, códigos, diplomático).

There are a few special rules when it comes to the written stress or accent mark in Spanish:

- One-syllable words never have a written accent except when there are two possible different meanings: el (the) and él (he), si (if) and sí (yes), tu (your) and tú (you), mas (but) and más (more).
- Some two-syllable words that might have two possible different meanings or functions in the sentence: solo (alone) and sólo (only), este (demonstrative adjective as in yo leo este libro/I read this book) and éste (demonstrative pronoun as in éste es mi libro/this is my book).
- Adverbs such as cuándo (when), dónde (where), and cómo (how) as well as pronouns such as quién (who), qué (what), and cuál (which) require an accent mark when used in questions and interrogatory sentences.

Capitalization

Capitalization is not used in Spanish as much as in English. The first word of a sentence is always capitalized. Proper names of people (Jorge Luis Borges, María), companies (Sony, Chevron) and places (España, Madrid, el río Nilo) are capitalized. Abbreviations of personal titles (Sr., Dr.) are capitalized but, if the full word is used, it is written in small case (el señor Aguilar, el doctor Fuentes). For titles of books, stories, poems, essays, songs, films, etc., only the first word is capitalized (La Guerra de las galaxias). The days of the week (lunes, viernes) and the months of the year (enero, abril) are not capitalized. Nationalities (argentino, australiano) and languages (latín, inglés) are not either.

Writing dates

In Spanish the days of the week and the months of the year are not capitalized unless they are at the beginning of a sentence. The proper way to write a date is 18 de diciembre de 1948 in contrast to the usual format of December 18, 1948 in English. However, the form diciembre 18, 1948 has started to show up in some places. When using dashes or slashes, the order is not the same: in English it is month/day/year while in Spanish is day/month/year. The correct meaning is obvious in some instance. There is no doubt that 25/12/2012 means December 25, 2012 as there is no 25th month. But in some cases it can be confusing. 3/7/2012 is July 3, 2012 in Spanish and March 7, 2012 in English. Be aware of this difference when reading and writing.

Writing numbers

The English language uses a period to denote the decimal point in a number and commas every 3 digits. In the Spanish language, it is just the opposite: a comma is used to denote the decimals and periods are used every 3 digits. The value of a penny would be written as 0.01 of a dollar in English and 0,01 of a dollar in Spanish. The number ten thousand will be written in English as 10,000, while in Spanish it will be 10.000. When writing or reading a definite number, the words hundred, thousand, and million in English are always in singular. In Spanish, the words cien and millón use the singular or the plural form in accordance with the number, while the word mil is always in singular (200 = doscientos; 1.000.000 = un millón, 5.000.000 = cinco millones; 3000 = tres mil).

Special Interrogation and exclamation marks

In Spanish, as in English, questions end with the interrogation mark (?), and exclamations end with the exclamation mark (!). But in Spanish for both types of sentences an inverted mark is require at the beginning. Therefore, all questions in Spanish begin with ¿, and all exclamations begin with ¡. Computer keyboards for the English language do not have a key for these symbols, and there are different options you can use to insert them depending on the program you are using. Familiarize yourself with the particular option you will have to use in the test.

Interrogative form

The structure of sentences denoting interrogation is very much the same in English and in Spanish. If the questions include interrogative adjectives, pronouns and adverbs such as quién, cuál, cómo, etc., the questions begins with those words (¿Quién vino?, ¿Cuál es tu casa?, ¿Cómo estás?). In all other cases the question will begin with the verb followed by the subject, as it is done in English (¿Llegaron los niños de la escuela?). Be aware that many times the subject is included in the verb and not specified otherwise (¿Llegaron de la escuela?). In their interrogative form, the interrogative adjectives, pronouns, and adverbs mentioned above always have a written stress or accent mark. Questions in Spanish require an interrogation mark at the beginning (¿) as well as at the end (?).

Exclamatory form

Exclamations in Spanish are usually expressed with qué in a very similar manner as English does with what (¡Qué día tan bonito!/What a beautiful day!) and how (¡Qué bonito!/How beautiful!). The exclamatory form is also use to denote a warning (¡Cuidado!/Careful!), an order (¡No hable!/Don't talk!) and emotions (¡Por fin llegaste!/You finally arrived!) in the same way as the English language does. As with interrogative adjectives, pronouns and adverbs such as qué, cómo, cuánto, etc., have a written stress or accent mark. In Spanish, also, all exclamations require an exclamation mark (¡) at the beginning as well as at the end (!).

Special cases for the spelling of conjunctions

For phonetic reasons, the conjunction y (and) changes to e when the word after the conjunction starts with i or hi (español e inglés, padre e hijo, Susana e Isabel). Something similar occurs with the conjunction o (or), which is changed to u when the word that follows it starts with o or ho (setenta u ochenta, casas u hoteles, Carlos u Honorio). When the conjunction but (pero) introduces a positive phrase that is contrary to the negative statement that precedes the conjunction, the conjunction used is sino (no quiero vino sino cerveza, no me gustan los perros sino los gatos, no hablamos con el director sino con su secretaria).

Changes in spelling for verbs ending in -uir

Verbs ending in -uir (incluir, huir, construir, contribuir, destruir) have a y in the present tense (yo incluyo, tú huyes, él construye, ellos contribuyen) before all endings except those beginning with an i (nosotros destruímos). The same rule applies for the past tense (él construyó, ellos contibuyeron, nosotros destruímos). The letter y in these words is pronounced like an i, except In Argentina and Uruguay where its sound is closer to the sh sound in English.

Spelling changes in verbs ending in -cer and -cir

Verbs in Spanish that end in -cer (conocer, parecer, merecer, ofrecer, crecer) or -cir (conducir, lucir, traducir, producir) preceded by a vowel are irregular in the present tense of the indicative for the

- 19 -

first person singular *yo*. These verbs have -zco as the ending for that particular tense and person (yo conozco, yo ofrezco, yo crezco, yo conduzco, yo traduzco, yo produzco). Similarly, in the present of the subjunctive tense, for all persons, these verbs use the ending -zca (que el merezca, que ellos aparezcan, que nosotros luzcamos). The same rules apply to all other verbs derived from those mentioned above (desconocer, desaparecer, aparecer, desmerecer, deslucir).

Spelling changes in verbs ending in -gar

The letter *g* in Spanish has always a hard sound before *a* (garúa), *o* (cargo), and *u* (gusano) but a soft sound before *e* (coger) and *i* (régimen). In those verbs ending in -gar (jugar, pagar, llegar), in order to keep the hard sound of the letter *g*, a *u* is added after the *g* for the first person singular form of the past tense (yo jugué, yo pagué, yo llegué), as well as in some subjunctive and imperative forms (jueguen, paguemos).

Spelling changes in verbs ending in -car

In Spanish, the letter *c* has a hard sound, like the letter *k* in English, when is it followed by an *a* (carro), *o* (colegio), or *u* (curva), and a soft sound like the *c* found in English in words such as century and cigar, when it is followed by the vowels *e* (celoso) or *i* (cien). To keep the hard sound of the letter *c* in the first person singular of the past tense of verbs ending in -car (sacar, tocar, buscar), the letter *c* is replaced by *qu* (yo saqué, yo toque, yo busqué) as well as in most subjunctive and imperative forms (toquemos, ¡no saques!).

Spelling changes in verbs ending in -ger and -gir

The letter *g* in Spanish always has a hard sound like the same letter in English in words such as garnet and gray before the letters *a* (gaviota), *o* (govierno), and *u* (agudo), but a soft sound before *e* (gerente) and *i* (agitar). In those verbs ending in -ger (escoger, recoger) and -gir (elegir, dirigir), to keep the soft sound for the first person singular in the present tense, the letter *g* is replaced by the letter *j*, which always has a soft sound (yo escojo, yo recojo, yo elijo, yo dirijo), as well as in all present subjunctive forms (que tú recojas, que elijamos), and negative commands (no elijas, no escojan).

Spelling changes in verbs ending in -zar

In Spanish, the letter *z* is never used before *e* or *i*; the letter *c* is used instead. Therefore verbs ending in -zar (empezar, alcanzar, utilizar), the *z* is replaced by a *c* for any conjugation ending in *e* (yo empecé, no alcances, que uds. utilicen). Also, because of this rule, there are no verbs ending in –zer or -zir.

Gender in Spanish words

There are two genders in Spanish, masculine and feminine, for nouns, adjectives, and articles. Every noun has a gender. There is no neutral (like *it* in English), and inanimate objects and other nouns that define similar concepts have a gender. There are no rules to determine which gender is assigned to each noun. With some exceptions, nouns that end with the letter *o* are masculine (carro, libro), and nouns that end with the letter *a* are feminine (casa, mesa). Nouns that refer to people or animals generally have the two versions: one ending in *a* for the female (niña, gata, perra), and one ending in *o* for the male (niño, gato, perro). Sometimes, as in English, the female and male of the same animated object use different nouns (woman/man, mujer/hombre) but the gender assignment is consistent with the gender they represent. The same rules apply to adjectives (casa cara/expensive house, libro caro/expensive book) and articles (las calles/the streets, los lápices/the pencils).

Word order in sentences

Both English and Spanish are basically SVO languages: languages in which the more common sentence structure is Subject + Verb + Object (The boy eats bread/El niño come pan). English is more structured and allows variations in word order mainly only for questions or in literature. Spanish is more flexible, and it is very common to find sentences where the verb or the object is at the beginning of the sentence (Pedro leyó este libro/Leyó Pedro este libro/Este libro lo leyó Pedro). The meaning of the sentence remains basically the same but with some subtle variations on emphasis. It is important to remark also that very often the subject is included in the verb in Spanish (Llegamos tarde/We arrived late).

Word derivatives

A derivate word is one that has been formed using an existing word as the basis. Derivatives are not variations of a word, like different conjugation forms of the same verb (eat/eats/eating) but new words (clear/clearly/unclear, respect/respectful/disrespect). The concept is the same in Spanish (persona/personalmente/impersonal, conocer/conocimiento/desconocer). In many cases, similar rules apply to English and Spanish. For example, deriving an adjective from an English noun ending in -tion by adding --al (recreation/recreational) is equivalent to replacing the -ción ending in a Spanish noun with -tivo to form an adjective (recreación/recreativo). Knowing the concept and the rules of derivation in Spanish is very useful to improve listening and comprehension skills, expand vocabulary, and increase fluency in the target language.

Instances where the same word is used both in Spanish and in English

All languages incorporate words and phrases from other languages. Spanish and English are no exceptions. English words related to technology have crossed over to a wide range of languages and words like e-mail, click, and DVD, for example, have been absorbed into Spanish, becoming a part of it. Spanish words have made their way into English, too. For some of them there is a translation (bodega/grocery store, fiesta/party, patio/courtyard), but many have no equivalent in English (adobe, armadillo, tango). Both languages also share the use of some French words (amateur, ballet, boulevard). Examples of loan words from Italian used both in English and Spanish include many musical terms (aria, cadenza, opera, piano, viola). And many of the words borrowed from German are used in philosophy in Spanish and in English (angst, ersatz, gestalt, geist).

Formal and informal forms of address

In English, there is only one second-person singular pronoun, you, for both formal and informal ways of addressing people. In Spanish, there are two forms: the formal usted and the informal tú. The informal tú has its own particular conjugation for all tenses (tú vienes, tú fuiste, tú comerás, tú has dormido). The informal tú also has its own set of possessive and reflexive pronouns (tu libro, tus hermanos, esta casa es tuya, Ana te invite al concierto). The formal usted, on the other hand, uses the same verb conjugations as the third-person singular pronoun él (usted viene, usted comerá, usted ha dormido). In a similar way, usted uses the third-person singular possessive and reflexive pronouns (su libro, sus hermanas, esta casa es suya, Ana lo invitó al concierto). In much of the Spanish speaking world, the second-person plural form for both formal and informal uses is ustedes, which shares its verb forms with ellos/ellas (ustedes tienen, ustedes vendrán, ustedes han comido). A few areas (such as Spain) differentiate between the formal and informal second-person plural, using ustedes formally , and vosotros informally (vosotros habláis, vosotros habéis visto, vosotros comisteis).

Vos as an informal form of address

In some areas of the world, such as Argentina and Bolivia, the informal second-person singular pronoun tú is very seldom used. Instead, these countries use vos. Vos has its own conjugations. For most tenses, these conjugations are the same as those of tú (tú comiste/vos comiste, tú has ido/vos has ido, tú comprarás/vos comprarás). The conjugations for vos are almost always different in the present indicative. In the case of regular verbs, the conjugation for vos is usually the same as tú, but with the stress on the last syllable (tú comes/vos comés, tú llegas/vos llegás). Exceptions abound with irregular verbs: tú vienes/vos venís, tú eres/vos sos, tú cierras/vos cerrás.

Conocer and saber

There are two different verbs in Spanish, that correspond to the infinitive phrase *to know* in English, conocer and saber. Saber is used when to know implies a mental effort, study, or training (she knows how to cook pasta/ella sabe cocinar pasta, he knows the lesson/él sabe la lección, they know to get to the school/ellos saben como llegar a la escuela). Conocer is used when to know denotes knowing through familiarity or acquaintance (he knows Mr. Jones/él conoce al Sr. Jones, she knows this part of the city/ella conoce esta parte de la ciudad).

Parecer

The verb parecer has different meanings in Spanish depending on whether it is used as a nonreflexive or reflexive verb. When used as a nonreflexive verb, it means to appear/to seem and expresses some level of uncertainty (el niño parece estar enfermo/the boy appears to be sick, parece que va a llover/it seems it is going to rain). Used as the reflexive verb parecerse, it means to resemble (Elena se parece a su hermano/Elena resembles her brother, dicen que yo me parezco mucho a mi padre/they say I resemble my father a lot).

Infinitive form

In English, the infinitive form of a verb is denoted by the marker *to* that precedes it. In Spanish, no marker precedes an infinitive, and the infinitive form is denoted by the endings ar (caminar, llorar, estar), er (correr, vender, ser), or ir (escribir, decir, ir). Each group has its own conjugation forms for all tenses, and they apply to all regular verbs that belong to that particular conjugation. Conjugated forms for irregular verbs vary from group to group and even within the same conjugation.

Expression hace...que

To describe an action that starts in the past and continues in the present, the Spanish language uses the present perfect tense (yo he estudiado español un año, Juan ha esperado dos horas, nosotros hemos vivido en esta ciudad muchos meses). Very often, these same type of ideas is expressed with hace ...que, which can be compared to the it's been in English (hace un año que yo estudio español, hace dos hora que Juan espera, hace muchos meses que nosotros vivimos en esta ciudad). When using hace...que, the sentence begins with hace, the time modifier, and then que, followed by the subject and verb, which is no longer in the present perfect of the indicative.

The verb haber:

	yo	tú	él	nosotros	ustedes	ellos
indicative present	he	has	ha	hemos	habéis	han
indicative imperfect	había	habías	había	habíamos	habíais	habían
indicative preterit	hube	hubiste	hubo	hubimos	hubisteis	hubieron
future	habré	habrás	habrá	habremos	habréis	habrán
conditional	habría	habrías	habría	habríamos	habríais	habrían
subjunctive present	haya	hayas	haya	hayamos	hayáis	hayan
subjunctive imperfect	hubiera/ hubiese	hubiera/ hubieses	hubiera/ hubiese	hubiéramos/ hubiésemos	hubierais/ hubieseis	hubieran/ hubiesen

In Spanish, the auxiliary verb used to form all perfect tenses is haber. It is an extremely irregular verb and has two different, interchangeable forms (hubiera/hubiese) for the imperfect of the subjunctive. Due to its importance as an auxiliary verb, all of its forms should be mastered. Haber is also used to form the past tense of deber (must) (John must have gone to the theater with Mary/John debe haber ido al teatro con Mary) and debía (should) (You should have called Susan last night/tú deberías haber llamado a Susan anoche) in those clauses that express probability. See the table on the opposite side for the conjugation of haber.

Quisiera

Quisiera and other forms of the imperfect subjunctive of querer are used very often in Spanish followed by an infinitive to express a polite request or desire and to soften a statement (yo quisiera hablar con usted, nosotros quisiéramos visitor Francia). It can be compared to "would like" in English (I would like to talk with you, we would like to visit France). If a different subject is introduced after quisiera (yo quisiera que usted...), then an infinitive clause cannot be used, and it must be replaced by a subordinate clause that uses the imperfect of the subjunctive (yo quisiera que usted me acompañara, Juan quisiera que el trabajo fuera más fácil).

Position of pronouns when using the present participle

The personal pronouns me, te, le, lo, la, nos, les, los, and las, when used as direct or indirect objects of a present participle are attached to the end of the present participle to form a single word (escribiéndome, escuchándote, mirándola, siguiéndonos). In the case of the progressive tenses with estar, there are two different and correct forms commonly used: the pronoun object can either be before the present participle as a separate word (Pedro me estaba diciendo, José te estaba leyendo el diario, Susana nos estaba esperando) or attached to the end of the participle (Pedro estaba esperándome, José estaba leyéndote el diario, Susana estaba esperándonos).

Reflexive verbs instead of the passive voice

The reflexive form of a verb is very commonly used in Spanish instead of the passive voice in those cases where the subject of the sentence is an inanimate object or when the performer of the action is not important or is not specified. This particular structure is more often used in the present tense. For example: *se vende carne en esa tienda* instead of *carne es vendida en esa tienda*; *se espera una gran lluvia* instead of *una gran lluvia es esperada*; *¿cómo se dice en español "grocery store"?* instead of *¿cómo es dicho "grocery store" en español?*

Most common reflexive verbs that have a different meaning in Spanish

There are several verbs in Spanish that have a different meaning, depending on whether they are used as reflexives verb or not. Parecer means to seem or to appear (parece que va a llover/it seems it is going to rain) while parecerse means to resemble (Juan se parece a su padres/Juan resembles his father). Dormir means to sleep (Ana duerme ocho horas por día/Ana sleeps eight hours per day) while dormirse means to fall asleep (Jorge se durmió en el tren/Jorge fell asleep in the train). Other examples are llamar (to call) and llamarse (to be named) and llevar (to carry) and llevarse (to get along).

Ojalá

The Spanish word ojalá does not have an exact translation in English. It is used to express a wish (ojalá supiera nadar/I wish I knew how to swim) or hope (ojalá que mañana sea un lindo día así podemos ir a la parque/I hope that tomorrow is a nice day so we can go to the park). In these cases, the world ojalá is always followed by the subjunctive (ojalá hubiera sabido esto ayer; ojalá lleguemos a tiempo; ojalá aprobemos el examen; ojalá hubiéramos salido más temprano).

Distributive adjectives and pronouns

While in English there are usually two different distributive adjectives and pronouns with the same meaning (each and every, everyone and everybody), in Spanish there is only one form for each particular connotation. Each and every are translated as cada (each season has its advantages/cada estación tiene sus ventajas; every passenger carried his suitcase/cada pasajero cargaba su maleta). The equivalent of everyone and everybody is todos (everyone loves him/todos lo aman; everybody was ready/todos estaban listos) and everything is todo (everything he said was true/todo lo que dijo era verdad).

Compound relative pronouns and the subjunctive

The compound relative pronouns quienquiera (whoever), cualquiera (whatever/whichever), and dondequiera (wherever) are always followed by que and then the verb in the subjunctive mode: quienquiera que escuche este sermon será transformado/whoever listens to this sermon will be transformed; este libro es útil para quienquiera que lo lea/this book is useful to whoever reads it; cualquiera que sea la causa, el resultado será el mismo/whatever the cause is, the result will be the same; dondequiera que él vaya, lo encontraremos/wherever he goes we will find him).

Different kinds of adverbs

Both in English and in Spanish, adverbs modify verbs, adjectives, other adverbs, and clauses (the bird flew high/el pájaro voló alto; the mountain is very high/la montaña es muy alta; the student knew the topic quite well/el estudiante sabía el tema bastante bien) in the same way adjectives modify nouns (it is a high mountain/es una montaña alta). There are several kinds of adverbs:

- of manner: rápidamente (quickly), bien (well), apropiadamente (appropriately)
- of place: aquí (here), allá (there), alrededor (around)
- of time: ahora (now), pronto (soon), hoy (today)
- of frequency: nunca (never), ocasionalmente (occasionally), a menudo (often)
- of degree: muy (very), bastante (quite), demasiado (too)
- interrogative: cuándo (when?), dónde (where?), por qué (why?)
- relative: cuando (when), donde (where), por que (why)

Equivalents in Spanish of Neither...nor and either...or

Spanish does not have two different words to express a combination of two alternative things. In the case of a negative connotation, it uses *ni* for both conjunctions neither and nor (neither the father nor the son are blond/ni el padre ni el hijo son rubios). Similarly, for affirmative or interrogative sentences, the Spanish language only uses *o* for both conjunctions either and or, (we can eat either meat or fish/podemos comer o carne o pescado; can I take either the train or the plane to go to Chicago?/¿puedo tomar o el tren o el avión para ir a Chicago?)

Equivalents in Spanish of some and any

In English, there are two different words to express the concept of a certain amount: some, which is used in affirmative sentences (we have some time), and any, which is used in negative and interrogative sentences (we don't have any ideas; do you have any brothers?). The Spanish language uses algún (alguna, algunos, algunas) o un poco de (tenemos algún/un poco de tiempo; ¿tienes algún hermano?) for affirmative and interrogative sentences, and ningún (ninguna, ningunos, ningunas) or nada de for negative sentences (no tenemos ninguna idea; no tenemos nada de cambio). The same rule applies to compound words formed with some and any. Spanish will use alguien (somebody/anybody), algo (something/anything), algún lugar (somewhere/anywhere, etc.) for the affirmative and interrogative forms, and nadie, nada, ningún lugar, etc., for the negative form.

Equivalents in Spanish of many/much and few/little

In English, many is used before countable nouns (many books, many things), and much before uncountable nouns (much money, much meat). The Spanish language does not differentiate between countable and uncountable nouns and uses only the word mucho. However, the ending of mucho will change according to the gender and number of the noun that follows (muchos libros, muchas cosas, mucho dinero, mucha carne). The same thing happens with few (few mistakes, few houses) and little (little time, little milk). In both cases they will be translated as poco, whose ending will agree in gender and number with the noun that follows (pocos errors, pocas casas, poco tiempo, poca leche).

Definite article

There is only one definite article in English, the, used to refer to something in a general way. It does not denote quantity or gender, being the same for singular, plural, feminine, and masculine nouns. By contrast, Spanish has different forms or variations depending on the characteristics of the noun. The masculine, singular form is el. The masculine, plural form is los. The feminine, singular form is la. The feminine, plural form is las. The definite article must always be in agreement in number and gender with the noun it precedes (el libro, la revista, los cigarros, las zanahorias). The definite article el does not have a written accent. When written with a stress mark, the word has a different meaning (él/he).

Conditional tense

The conditional tense in Spanish is used in the same way the conditional is used in English:

- with the subjunctive in true conditional if clauses (si yo fuera Juan, no iría a la fiesta/if I were Juan, I wouldn't go to the party; si lloviera, el jardín no se vería tan feo/if it rained, the garden wouldn't look so ugly)

- in indirect speech, when the main verb is in the past and the second verb denotes a future action in the past (Juan dijo que hablaría con ella/Juan said he would talk with her; Pedro me informó que iría al cine/Pedro informed me he would go to the movies)

Diminutives

Diminutives are used to denote smallness or to express affection, and are usually formed in Spanish by adding the suffix ito at the end of the noun. If the noun ends in an unaccented vowel, the vowel is dropped (libro/librito; perro/perrito). If the noun ends in e, n, or r, a c is added to the suffix (padre/padrecito; joven/jovencito; mujer/mujercita). The suffix has to agree with the gender and number of the noun (camión/camioncito; collares/collarcitos; blusa/blusita; silla/sillitas). Other spelling changes that need to be taken into account are for nouns that have g or c in the last syllable; they change to gu and qu (lago/laguito; Paco/Paquito).

Relative pronouns cuyo and donde

The relative pronoun *cuyo* in Spanish is equivalent to whose or of which in English. *Cuyo* has to agree with the gender and number of the noun it modifies, not with the subject that executes the action (la película cuyo director ganó el premio/the movie whose director won the prize; el escritor cuyas novelas leímos en clase/the writer whose novels we read in class).

The relative pronoun donde in Spanish is equivalent to where or which in English and does not have a written accent (la casa donde conocí a Roberto/the house where I met Robert; la puerta por donde salió María/the door through which Mary left).

Conjunctions that sometimes require the subjunctive

Some conjunctions such as aunque, como, donde, de manera que, de modo que, según, and mientras, when used to express the opinion of the speaker, uncertainty or a conjecture, require the use of the subjunctive mode (aunque tengamos el dinero, no vamos a comprar un auto nuevo/even though we may have the money—we are not sure we do—we are not going to buy a new car; comemos donde tú quieras/we'll eat where you want—but we do not know where you want to eat). In all other cases, they are followed by the indicative.

Conjunctions that always require the subjunctive

The conjunctions antes (de) que, para que, sin que, a fin de que, a menos que, con tal (de) que, and en caso de que are always followed by the verb in the subjunctive (termina el trabajo antes de que el jefe te lo pida; voy a visitarte para que podamos hablar; hicimos el trabajo sin que ella se diera cuenta; apagué la televisión a fin de que pudieras estudiar; a menos que tengas otra idea, vayamos al cine; con tal de que vengas, no me importa la hora; en caso de que venga el plomero, aquí dejo el dinero para pagarle).

Cognates

Cognates are words in different languages that have the same etymological origin and similar meaning, spelling, and pronunciation. Some are identical (doctor, terrible, hospital, cruel) and some have minor differences (religion/religión, Canada/Canadá, novel/novela, dentist/dentista, president/presidente, information/ información). Other cognates have larger differences but still have the same root (abandonar/abandon, decidir/decide, universidad/university). False cognates are words that have some similarities in spelling and pronunciation but do not share the same origins and do not have the same meaning (exit/salida—éxito/success, hay/heno—hay/there is, large/grande—largo/long, pie/pastel—pie/foot, rope/soga—ropa /clothes, embarrassed/avergonzada—embarazada/pregnant, fabric/tela—fábrica/factory, library/biblioteca—librería/bookstore).

Possessive adjectives

In Spanish, possessive adjectives refer to the possessor but have to agree also in gender and number with the noun they modify (mi hijo, mis hijos; nuestra casa, nuestras casas). Be aware that Spanish uses the same possessive adjective su for the third person regardless of the gender and number of the possessor (Susan's son—su hijo; Peter's house—su casa; my sisters' books—sus libros; the dogs' food—su comida). Su is also used for the formal second person singular (you brought your book/usted trajo su libro) and for the second person plural (you drink your coffee/ustedes toman su café).

Possessive pronouns

Possessive pronouns in Spanish have the same functions as their English equivalent: they replace a possessive adjective and a noun, and are most commonly used to put emphasis in ownership (the dog is mine/el perro es mío). Possessive pronouns have to be in accordance in gender and number with the noun they are replacing (la casa es nuestra, los libros son tuyos, las sillas son suyas, los lápices son míos). As with the possessive adjectives, the possessive pronoun suyo is used for the third person regardless of gender or number, the formal second person singular, and the second person plural.

The preposition *para*

The prepositions for and to can be translated as *para*. *Para* is used in the following instances:

- Direction or destination (tenemos que salir para la oficina/we have to leave for the office)
- Recipient of something (compré esta blusa para mi hermana/I bought this blouse for my sister)
- Purpose (el plomero vino para arreglar la ducha/the plumber came to fix the shower)
- Time/deadline (siempre vamos a la casa de mis padres para Navidad/we always go to my parents' house for Christmas)
- Comparison (la mesa es demasiado grande para la cocina/the table is too big for the kitchen)
- Intended use (el día es para trabajar/the day is for working)

The preposition *por*

In some instance the preposition for is translated as *por*. *Por* is also used to replace through, by, and per. Por is used in the following instances:

- Means of transportation or communication (lo llamo por teléfono/I call him by phone, voy a Madrid por avión/I go to Madrid by plane)
- Exchange/substitution (cambié la blusa grande por una mediana/I exchanged the large blouse for a medium)
- Duration (los niños jugaron por cuatro horas/the children play for four hours)
- Quantity (ella gana $400 por semana/she earns $400 per week)
- Object of an errand (voy al mercado por la leche/I go to the market for milk)
- Agent (el libro fue escrito por Pedro/the book was written by Pedro)

- 27 -

Demonstrative adjectives

In Spanish there are three possible demonstrative adjectives: *este*, *ese*, and *aquel*, compared to the two that exist in English (this, that). *Este* refers to anything close. *Ese* denotes a certain distance. *Aquel* indicates farther away or over there. Demonstrative adjectives, like all adjectives in Spanish, have to agree in gender and number with the nouns they modify (este libro/this book; aquella casa/the house over there; esos gatos/those cats; estas sillas/these chairs).

Demonstrative pronouns

In Spanish there are three possible demonstrative pronouns (éste, ése, aquél) compared to the two that exist in English (this one, that one), and they do not have the word one following them as in English (this one/éste). They have the same form as the demonstrative adjectives (este) but with a written accent (éste). Demonstrative pronouns have to agree in gender and number with the noun they refer to. (blusa—ésta; libro—éste; casas—éstas; perros—éstos). There is also a neutral form (esto, eso, aquello). They do not have a written accent, and they usually refer to ideas or general phrases (¿por qué dices eso?/why do you say that?; no hay nada peor que esto/there is nothing worse than this).

Possession

Spanish does not have the *'s* to express possession. It uses the preposition *de* instead (Tom's book/el libro de Tom; my parents' house/la casa de mis padres). In many instances *de* is followed by the definite article. In those cases, the article has to agree in gender and number with the noun that follows (el libro de la niña; el gato de los vecinos). For phonetic reasons when *de* is followed by *el*, the two words are contracted into *del* (el libro del niño). To inquire about possession, de quién is equivalent to whose (¿de quién es este libro?/whose book is this?). In those cases where you know there is more than one possessor, de quiénes is used in the interrogative form (¿de quienes son estos libros?/whose books are these?). In the interrogative form, there is no difference between feminine and masculine.

Adjectives

Adjectives in Spanish have to be in accordance in gender and number with the nouns they modify. Similar rules used to account for gender and number for nouns also apply to adjectives. Adjectives end in *a* for feminine and *o* for masculine (niña bonita/niño bonito). To form the plural an *s* is added to adjectives ending in a vowel (mesa verde/mesas verdes) and *es* (libro azul/libros azules) to those ending in a consonant. Those adjectives ending in *e* use the same form for both genders (casa grande/avión grande). Adjectives are usually put after the noun they modify.

Adjectives that go before the noun

In Spanish, adjectives are usually placed after the noun they modify. Exceptions are those adjectives that denote quantity such as *alguno, ambos, bastante, mucho, poco, suficiente, varios* (presentó algunas ideas; ambos estudiantes son alemanes; tengo bastante dinero; hace mucho calor; hay poca comida; tenemos suficiente tiempo; visitamos varias ciudades); and adjectives that refer to order such as *primero, segundo*, etc. (la segunda casa a la derecha). Some adjectives that indicate quality such as *bueno, malo, mejor* and *peor* can be before or after the noun (buena comida/comida buena; el peor caso/el caso peor). In most cases, if the adjective ends in *o*, the *o* is dropped if the adjective precedes the noun (mal libro; buen restaurante; primer piso; algun tiempo).

- 28 -

Adjectives before or after the noun

Be aware some adjectives have different meanings depending on whether they are before or after the noun they modify. Some examples are:

- la antigua capital/the former capital—la capital antigua/the old capital
- una cierta condición/a certain condition—una condición cierta/a sure condition
- diferentes ideas/various ideas—ideas diferentes/different ideas
- gran universidad/great university—universidad grande/big university
- el mismo jefe/the same boss—el jefe mismo/the boss himself
- pobre hombre/man who deserves pity—hombre pobre/destitute man
- un simple carpintero/just a carpenter—un carpintero simple/a simple carpenter
- la única oportunidad/the only opportunity—la oportunidad única/the unique opportunity

Adverb formation

In Spanish, to form an adverb from an adjective, the suffix *-mente* is added to the feminine, singular form of the adjective (rápido/rápidamente; lento/lentamente). This is similar to the addition of -ly to an adjective to form an adverb in English (quick/quickly; sad/sadly). Adjectives that are the same in the feminine and in the masculine just add *-mente* to its singular form (fácil/fácilmente; triste/tristemente). Adverbs that refer to volume (alto, bajo, fuerte) use the masculine singular and do not add *-mente* (hablar alto). *Demasiado, más, menos, mucho, poco, mejor, peor,* and *tanto* do not change (vayamos más rápido; es el sitio peor iluminado). The adverb that corresponds to *bueno* is *bien*, and to *malo* is *mal* (el hotel está bien ubicado).

Indefinite article

The equivalent of the English indefinite article a/an and its plural some/a few in Spanish is *un*. It has to agree in gender and number with the noun it precedes (un libro, una revista, unos libros, unas revistas). The use of the indefinite article is very similar in both languages, although there are some differences. In general, when talking about religion and profession, there is no need of an indefinite article in Spanish (Pedro es católico/Pedro is a Catholic; Juan es médico/Juan is a doctor) unless an adjective also modifies the noun (Pedro es un católico devoto/Pedro is a devout Catholic; Juan es un médico excelente/Juan is an excellent doctor).

Adverbs and their position in the sentence

There are some rules regarding the position of an adverb in a sentence:

- adverbs of manner always follow the verb they modify (los chicos jugaron bien el partido)
- adverbs cannot be placed between an auxiliary verb and the principal verb (el hermano ha destruído totalmente el castillo de arena de Paula)
- a direct object is placed between the verb and the adverb (el artista cantó la canción elegantemente)
- when there is more than one adverb ending in *-mente*, only the last one adds it, the other ones use the feminine, singular form of the adjective (me lo explicó claro y completamente)

The relative pronoun *que*

Relative pronouns connect two independent sentences. *Que*, which stands for that, who, or whom, is the most common relative pronoun in Spanish. *Que* introduces the relative or dependent clause.

Leo un libro. El libro es interesante—El libro que leo es interesante./The book that I read is interesting.

Las maestras trabajan en esta escuela. Las maestras son buenas.—Las maestras que trabajan en esta escuela son buenas./The teachers who work in this school are good.

In English, you can sometimes omit the relative pronoun (the house I like/the house that I like). This omission is not accepted in Spanish (la casa que me gusta).

Nouns and their number

The process to form the plural of a noun from the singular version is very similar in Spanish and English, and consists mainly of adding an *s* at the end of the word. In Spanish, the rule applies to all nouns ending in a vowel (libro/libros; hermana/hermanas). When the noun ends in a consonant, instead of adding an *s*, the noun is pluralized but adding *es* (mes/meses; ley/leyes; árbol/árboles, pescador/pescadores) just as it is done in English with words that end in s (process/processes). Be aware of required spelling changes when adding *es* (pez/peces; lapiz/lápices).

Nouns, special plurals

Some nouns, such as *anteojos* (glasses) and *tijeras* (scissors), are always used in plural in Spanish. Others, such as *afueras* (outskirts), *ganas* (willingness), and *bienes* (assets), are generally used in the plural but might be occasionally used in the singular. Nouns that have more than one syllable and end with an unstressed vowel plus an *s* do not have a different form for the plural (la crisis/las crisis; el jueves/los jueves; el paraguas/los paraguas). Family names are not pluralized (la familia García vive en esta casa/the García family lives in this house—mi hermana conoce a los García/my sister knows the Garcías)

Agreement

In Spanish, the article and the adjective used with a noun must agree in gender and number with the noun they refer to (el coche rojo, los coches rojos, la blusa amarilla, las blusas amarillas). The subject of the sentence and the verb associated with that subject have to agree in person and number (el niño lloró; los niños lloraron; yo tengo frío; nosotros tenemos frío; tú vienes esta noche; ustedes vienen esta noche). There are also rules for the agreement of verb tenses and modes depending on the type of sentence, especially for conditional phrases (Si Juan se sacara la lotería, él se compraría un coche nuevo).

Nouns and their gender, special rules

There are some special rules regarding the gender of nouns:

- nouns ending in *dad, tad, tud, umbre, ión, ie, cia, ez,* and *eza* are usually feminine (la ciudad, la libertad, la certidumbre, la canción, la serie, la diferencia, la sencillez, la tristeza)
- nouns ending in *aje, ambre, or,* and *án* are usually masculine (el equipaje, el calambre, el valor, el refrán)

Other groups of nouns that are masculine are:

- the days of the week (el martes, el jueves)
- the months of the year (el enero, el agosto)
- languages (el griego, el inglés)

- numbers (el uno, el diez)
- colors (el gris, el blanco)
- infinitives (el contaminar, el caminar)
- rivers, seas, and oceans (el río Nilo, el mar Rojo, el océano Pacífico)

Nouns, other rules to form the feminine

There are some other rules used in Spanish to from the feminine of a noun:

- nouns that end in or, *án, ón,* and *ín* are usually masculine and form the feminine by adding an *a* (doctor/doctora; alemán/alemana; campeón/campeona; bailarín/bailarina).
- nouns ending in *e, ista,* and *nte* stay the same in both the feminine and the masculine forms (el agente/la agente; el artista/la artista; el cantante/la cantante).

Some nouns have the same form for the feminine and the masculine, but their meaning is different depending on the gender (el capital/money—la capital/city; el frente/front—la frente/forehead; el orden/neatness—la orden/command; el policía/policeman—la policía/police force but also policewoman)

Comparison, superiority and inferiority

In most cases, comparisons in Spanish are denoted by the expressions *más...que* and *menos...que* with the adjective, adverb, or noun placed in between (Juan es más grande que Pedro; yo trabajo más rápidamente que Tomás; tenemos más confianza que tú; mi jardín está menos iluminado que el del vecino; Susana tiene menos dinero que Ana). Some exceptions are *menor* (younger), *mayor* (older), *mejor* (better), and *peor* (worse) (yo soy menor que mi hermano; mi hermano es mayor que yo; Pedro tiene mejor voz que Juan; Juan tiene peor voz que Pedro).

Comparison, equality

To express a comparison of equality, the Spanish language uses the expression *tan...como* with the adjective or adverb in between (Juan es tan alto como Pedro; Juan escribe tan bien como Pedro). If the comparison includes a noun, the expression *tanto...como* is used (este vaso tiene tanto jugo como ése). In this expression, *tanto* has to agree in gender and number with the noun it refers to (tengo tanto frío como ustedes; Juan tiene tantos juguetes como Pedro; la montaña recibió tanta lluvia como el valle; tengo tantas hermanas como Juan).

Relative superlative

The relative superlative applies to a noun in the context of a group. The superlative degree of adjectives in Spanish is expressed by using the comparative form of the adjective (más lindo, menos inteligente) preceded by the definitive article (el más lindo, el menos inteligente). The definite article has to agree in gender and number with the noun it refers to (María es la más bonita de las hermanas; Pedro y Juan son los menos autoritarios del grupo; estas casas son las más caras de la zona). This rule also applies to the irregular comparatives such as *mejor* (best), *peor* (worst), *mayor* (oldest), and *menor* (youngest) (la mejor carne de la región; el peor alumno de la clase, las mayores distancias del país; los menores detalles de la pintura).

Absolute superlative

The absolute superlative is the very or extremely in English and does not describe a noun within the context of a group. One way to denote the absolute superlative in Spanish is by adding *muy* or

- 31 -

extremadamente before the adjective (Pedro es muy inteligente; Juan es extremadamente cuidadoso). Another option is to add the suffix *-ísimo* to the adjective (Pedro es inteligentísimo) in accordance in gender and number with the noun it refers to (ísima, ísimos, ísimas). Adjectives ending in a vowel lose it when the suffix is added (mucho/muchísimo; cara/carísima; malos/malísimos; pequeños/pequeñísimos). Be aware of spelling changes required to comply with spelling rules (rico/riquísimo; largo/larguísimo; feliz/felicísimo).

Gustar

The infinitive *to like* in Spanish requires a different sentence structure than English. In English the word order is the person (subject), the verb, and then the object (I like this book). In Spanish an indirect personal pronoun goes first (representing the person), then the verb, and then the object, which is actually the subject of the sentence (Me gusta este libro). A literal translation of the sentence in English would be: This book is pleasing to me. Other verbs that require the same sentence structure as gustar are: molestar (me molestan los zapatos/the shoes bother me); aburrir (nos aburre la música clasica/classical music bores us); encantar (le encanca cantar/he loves to sing), fascinar; faltar; and interesar.

Ser and estar

Ser and *estar* correspond to the infinitive phrase *to be* in English. *Ser* is used to describe something that is intrinsic to a person, object, or idea, such as nationality (Marta es argentina), origin (la carne es de vaca), identification (Pedro es mi hijo), physical characteristics (soy rubia), generalities (somos estudiantes), dates (hoy es 12 de octubre), time of the day (son las diez de la noche), place of events—where something is occurring— (la fiesta es en mi casa), possession (la casa es mía), and personality traits (Ana es simpática). *Ser* is very irregular; see the table below for its conjugation for the simple tenses of the indicative.

	Present	Imperfect	Preterit
yo	soy	era	fui
tú	eres	eras	fuiste
él	es	era	fue
nosotros	somos	éramos	fuimos
vosotros	sois	erais	fuisteis
ellos	son	eran	fueron

Ser and *estar* correspond to the verb to be in English. Estar is used to describe a condition and sometimes is considered less permanent, about a person, object, or idea. It is used to describe location or position—where something is—(el libro está sobre la mesa; Juan está en Nueva York), physical appearance—i.e. how someone looks— (Susana está bonita con ese vestido), and emotional state (Pedro está contento), as well as actions in progress (María está cocinando; nosotros estamos tomando cerveza). The verb *estar* is very irregular; see the table below for its conjugation for the simple tenses of the indicative.

	Present	Imperfect	Preterit
yo	estoy	estaba	estuve
tú	estás	estabas	estuviste
él	está	estaba	estuvo
nosotros	estamos	estábamos	estuvimos
vosotros	estais	estabais	estuvisteis
ellos	están	estaban	estuvieron

Informal commands

Affirmative commands for *tú* (salta más alto/jump higher) are formed with the present of the indicative conjugation of the third person singular (él salta). When needed, direct personal pronouns can be added at the end of the verb (llámame más tarde/call me later). Be aware that the addition of the pronoun changes the structure of the word and usually requires a written accent or stress mark. Negative informal commands are formed using the present of the subjunctive (no hables tan fuerte/don't talk so loud). *No* is always placed before the verb. Negative informal commands use the direct or indirect personal pronoun as a separate word between *no* and the verb (no me llames esta noche/don't call me tonight).

Past participles

Past participles can be used as adjectives. When used as such, the past participle has to agree in gender and number with the noun it modifies (librería cerrada, consultorio cerrado, tiendas cerradas, edificios cerrados). To form the past participle of regular –*ar* verbs, drop the ending -*ar* and add -*ado* (hablar/hablado); for –*er/-ir* verbs, drop the ending -*er* or -*ir* and add -*ido* (comer/comido, dormir/dormido). –*Er* and –*ir* verbs that have an *a, e,* or *o* before the ending of the infinitive require a written accent in their past participles (caer/caído; sonreir/sonreído; oir/oído).

Irregular verbs with an unexpected *g*

Some verbs have an unexpected *g* in the first person singular of the present of the indicative while they follow the normal conjugation rules for the rest of the forms (hacer/yo hago, tú haces, él hace, nosotros hacemos, ustedes hacen, ellos hacen). Other verbs have the unexpected g but have other irregularities in other persons too (decir/yo digo, tú dices, él dice, nosotros decimos, ustedes dicen, ellos dicen). *Caer, poner, salir, traer,* and *valer* belong to the first group. *Oir, tener, venir,* and their various forms belong to the second group.

Present perfect

The present perfect tense denotes an action in the recent past and is generally used in Spanish the same way it is used in English. It is formed with the present of the indicative of the auxiliary verb haber (yo he, tú has, él ha, nosotros hemos, vosotros habéis, ellos han) and the past participle of the verb (yo he comido bien hoy; tú has viajado a Nueva York este mes; ella ha hecho la tarea esta mañana; nosotros hemos hablado con el director esta semana; ustedes han vivido aquí todo el año; ellos han dormido poco esta noche).

Present indicative

Drop the infinitive ending of the verb and use the endings in the table below to form the present of the indicative for all regular verbs.

	AR	ER	IR
yo	-o	-o	-o
tú	-as	-es	-es
él	-a	-e	-e
nosotros	-amos	-emos	-imos
vosotros	-ais	-eis	-ís
ellos	-an	-en	-en

Examples:

- hablar/yo hablo; caminar/tú caminas; viajar/él viaja; regresar/nosotros regresamos; cepillar/vosotros cepilláis; llamar/ellos llaman
- comer/yo como; aprender/tú aprendes; correr/él corre; desparecer/nosotros desaparecemos; beber/vosotros bebéis; depender/ellos dependen
- vivir/yo vivo; escribir/tú escribes; recibir/él recibe; acudir/nosotros acudimos; batir/vosotros batís; percibir/ellos perciben

The verb *ir*

The verb *ir* is used as an auxiliary verb in Spanish as the "going to" expression in English and to form the continuous tenses (voy a comer a las 2; ellos iban a completar la tarea anoche). The verb *ir* is irregular. See the table below for its conjugation for the simple tenses of the indicative.

	Present	Imperfect	Preterit
yo	voy	iba	fui
tú	vas	ibas	fuiste
él	va	iba	fue
nosotros	vamos	íbamos	fuimos
vosotros	vais	ibais	fuisteis
ellos	van	iban	fueron

El pretérito

Drop the infinitive ending of the verb and use the endings in table below to form the preterit of the indicative for all regular verbs (*-ar, -er,* and *–ir*).

	AR	ER	IR
yo	-é	-í	-í
tú	-aste	-iste	-iste
él	-ó	-ió	-ió
nosotros	-amos	-imos	-imos
vosotros	-asteis	-isteis	-isteis
ellos	-aron	-ieron	-ieron

Examples:

- hablar/yo hablé; caminar/tú caminaste; viajar/él viajó; regresar/nosotros regresamos; cepillar/vosotros cepillasteis; llamar/ellos llamaron
- comer/yo comí; aprender/tú aprendiste; correr/él corrió; desparecer/nosotros desaparecimos; beber/vosotros bebisteis; depender/ellos dependieron
- vivir/yo viví; escribir/tú escribiste; recibir/él recibió; acudir/nosotros acudimos; batir/vosotros batisteis; percibir/ellos percibieron

- 34 -

Imperfect

The imperfect is used to express:

- habitual actions in the past (cuando era niño, siempre jugaba en el parque; siempre íbamos de vacaciones a Canadá)
- age in the past (tenía 9 años cuando conocí a Pedro; ¿cuántos años tenías cuando entraste a la escuela)
- time in the past (¿qué hora era cuando empezó el partido?; eran las nueve de la noche cuando llegué a casa)
- physical and emotional characteristics (Ana era muy alta de niña; mi tío era un hombre muy simpático; Luís estaba muy contento)
- continuous actions interrupted by another action in the past (yo leía una novela cuando sonó el teléfono; Juan dormía cuando empezó el incendio)

Past imperfect

Drop the infinitive ending of the verb and use the endings in the table below to form the preterit of the indicative for all regular verbs.

	AR	ER	IR
yo	-aba	-ía	-ía
tú	-abas	-ías	-ías
él	-aba	-ía	-ía
vosotros	-ábais	-íais	-íais
ustedes	-aban	-ían	-ían
ellos	-aban	-ían	-ían

nosotros
-ábamos
-íamos

Examples:

- hablar/yo hablaba; caminar/tú caminabas; viajar/él viajaba; regresar/nosotros regresábamos; cepillar/vosotros cepillábais; llamar/ellos llamaban
- comer/yo comía; aprender/tú aprendías; correr/él corría; desparecer/nosotros desaparecíamos; beber/vosotros bebíais; depender/ellos dependían
- vivir/yo vivía; escribir/tú escribías; recibir/él recibía; acudir/nosotros acudíamos; batir/vosotros batíais; percibir/ellos percibían

Future of the indicative

To form the future of the indicative of all regular verbs, add the endings shown in the table below to the infinitive, regardless of the conjugation -ar, -er, or -ir.

	Future
yo	-é
tú	-ás
él	-á
nosotros	-eremos
vosotros	-éis
ellos	-eran

Examples:

- hablar/yo hablaré; caminar/tú caminarás; viajar/él viajará; regresar/nosotros regresaremos; cepillar/vosotros cepillaréis; llamar/ellos llamarán
- comer/yo comeré; aprender/tú aprenderás; correr/él correrá; desparecer/nosotros desapareceremos; beber/vosotros beberéis; depender/ellos dependerán
- vivir/yo viviré; escribir/tú escribirás; recibir/él recibirá; acudir/nosotros acudiremos; batir/vosotros batiréis; percibir/ellos percibirán

Conditional tense

To form the conditional of all regular verbs, add the endings shown in the table below to the infinitive, regardless of the conjugation *-ar, -er,* or *-ir.*

	Conditional
yo	-ía
tú	-ías
él	-ía
nosotros	-íamos
vosotros	-íais
ellos	-ían

Examples:

- hablar/yo hablaría; caminar/tú caminarías; viajar/él viajaría; regresar/nosotros regresaríamos; cepillar/vosotros cepillaríais; llamar/ellos llamarían
- comer/yo comería; aprender/tú aprenderías; correr/él correría; desparecer/nosotros desapareceríamos; beber/vosotros beberíais; depender/ellos depenerían
- vivir/yo viviría; escribir/tú escribirías; recibir/él recibiría; acudir/nosotros acudiríamos; batir/vosotros batiríais; percibir/ellos percibirían

Perfect tenses and their uses

The present perfect is used to denote an action that took place at an indefinite period in the past (yo he leído este libro/I have read this book) or to describe a past action that continues into the present time (hemos vivido aquí muchos años/we have lived here many years).

The past perfect of the indicative is used to denote an action in the past that happened before the second action in the past (cuando me desperté, Marta ya había llegado/when I woke up, Marta had already arrived).

The future perfect is used to denote an action that will be completed in the future before a certain time or another action in the future occurs (me habré graduado antes de ir de vacaciones/I will have graduated before going on vacation).

The conditional perfect is used to denote an action that would have been completed in the past under certain conditions (ella le habría dicho la verdad/she would have told him the truth)

Progressive tenses

Progressive tenses use the verb *estar* as an auxiliary verb with the present participle of the main verb (yo estoy comiendo/I am eating; tú estás durmiendo/you are sleeping; él está estudiando/he is studying; nosotros estamos viniendo/we are coming; vosotros estáis trabajando/you are working; ellos están cocinando/they are cooking). The progressive tenses are used to denote an action that is or was in progress (yo estaba durmiendo/I was sleeping; nosotros estuvimos mirando/we were watching). Progressive tenses are never used in reference to the future ("going to" in English). For those cases, Spanish uses *ir a* and the infinitive of the main verb (I am going to do my homework/voy a hacer mi tarea; they are going to finish the book/ellos van a terminar el libro).

Present participle

The present participle (the -ing form in English) is formed in Spanish by dropping the infinitive ending of the verb and adding *-ando* (caminar/caminando; trabajar/trabajando) for *–ar* verbs and *-iendo* for *–er/-ir* verbs (comer/comiendo, correr/corriendo; salir/saliendo; recibir/recibiendo). *–Er/-ir* verbs with irregularities in the present of the indicative usually have an irregular present participle (dormir/durmiendo; creer/creyendo; poder/pudiendo; ir/yendo). The present participle is used in Spanish in largely the same way it is used in English.

Formal commands

Affirmative commands for *usted* (salte más alto/jump higher) are formed with the present of the subjunctive of the third person singular (él hable). When needed, direct/indirect pronouns are added at the end of the verb (llámeme más tarde/call me later, hágalo ahora). Be aware that the addition of the pronoun changes the syllabic structure of the word and requires a written accent or stress mark. Negative informal commands simply add *no* before the verb (no hable tan fuerte/don't talk so loud). *No* is always placed before the verb. Negative formal commands, like informal commands, use the direct/indirect pronoun as a separate word between *no* and the verb (no me llame esta noche/don't call me tonight, no lo haga)

Que and quien

Que is used in Spanish as a relative pronoun in reference to persons, objects, and ideas, both for the singular and for the plural (la persona que llamó por teléfono; los niños que jugaban en el parque; los libros que encargué; la admiración que sentía por su padre). If the pronoun is preceded by a preposition, then *quien* must be used instead of *que* when referring to persons (la amiga con quien fui al cine ayer; el hombre a quien ví en la oficina). Sometimes *quien* is used instead of *que* for more clarity (hablé con la maestro nueva, quien estaba muy contenta). *Quien* has to agree in number with its antecedent (las niñas, quienes habían dormido hasta tarde, estaban desayunando)

Cual

In those cases where the use of *que* as a relative pronoun may create confusion or ambiguity, *que* is replace by *el cual* (el primo de mi amigo, el cual vive en Miami, se fue de vacaciones). *El cual* takes the form *la cual, los cuales,* and *las cuales* to agree in gender and number with its antecedent (la mesa, encima de la cual puso las flores, es de madera; ellos tienen cuatro hijos, dos de los cuales viven en Houston; las pinturas, las cuales viste en el museo, se vendieron muy bien). *El cual* is also used after the *prepositions por, sin, después de, además de, contra, detrás,* and *hacia.*

Subjunctive

The subjunctive is used in subordinate clauses introduced by *que* to express:

- a wish (quiero que Juan venga a la fiesta),
- uncertainty or doubt (es probable que María se case con Juan),
- a command (dígale al chofer que esté aquí a las seis),
- an emotion (es una lástima que ustedes no puedan venir a visitarnos),
- preference or need (es mejor que te pongas un abrigo),
- approval/disapproval (está bien que te vistas de negro para el funeral)

The subjunctive is also used with adverbial clauses introduced by the following conjuctions *cuando, antes que, hasta que, tan pronto como, mientras, para que, afin de que, de manera que, sin que, aunque, a menos que,* and *con tal que* (quiero hablar con Pedro tan pronto como llegue; continúen con el trabajo a menos que el jefe diga lo contrario).

Present of the subjunctive

To form the present of the subjunctive of regular verbs, take the first person singular of the present of the indicative (yo hablo), drop the o, and add the endings shown in the table below.

	AR	ER/IR
yo	-e	-a
tú	-es	-as
él	-e	-a
nosotros	-emos	-amos
vosotros	-éis	-áis
ellos	-en	-an

Examples:

- hablar/yo hable; caminar/tú camines; viajar/él viaje; regresar/nosotros regresemos; cepillar/vosotros cepilléis; llamar/ellos llamen
- comer/yo coma; aprender/tú aprendas; correr/él corra; entender/nosotros entendamos; beber/vosotros bebáis; depender/ellos dependan
- vivir/yo viva; escribir/tú escribas; recibir/él reciba; acudir/nosotros acudamos; batir/vosotros batáis; percibir/ellos perciban

Imperfect of the subjunctive

To form the imperfect of the subjunctive of regular verbs, take the third person plural of the preterit of the indicative (ellos hablaron), drop ron, and add the endings shown in the table below.

	AR/ER/IR
yo	-ra
tú	-ras
él	-ra
nosotros	-ramos
vosotros	-rais
ellos	-ran

- 38 -

Examples:

- hablar/yo hablara; caminar/tú caminaras; viajar/él viajara; regresar/nosotros regresáramos; cepillar/vosotros cepillarais; llamar/ellos llamaran
- comer/yo comiera; aprender/tú aprendieras; correr/él corriera; entender/nosotros entendiéramos; beber/vosotros bebierais; depender/ellos dependieran
- vivir/yo viviera; escribir/tú escribieras; recibir/él recibiera; acudir/nosotros acudiéramos; batir/vosotros batierais; percibir/ellos percibieran

Cultural Perspectives, Comparisons, and Connections

Sociolinguistics

Sociolinguistics studies the relationships between language and society, how they interact, and how they modify and impact each other. Language changes and is modified by features such as geographical location, socioeconomic class, education level, age group, gender, ethnicity, and contact with or knowledge of other languages. These elements affect all languages to various degrees depending on the particular social factors, constantly altering different parts of the language such as pronunciation, word choice, and sentence structure. With Spanish spoken in so many different countries, geographical location is one of the most significant sociolinguistic factors that affect it, and it is very important to pay attention to the local nuances.

Metric and imperial measurement systems

Spanish speaking countries mostly use the metric system for all measurements. Although some units such as those of time (seconds/segundos, hours/horas, days/días, etc.) and angles (degrees/grados) are the same, other units are different. For longitude and distances, Spanish use centimeters (centímetros), meters (metros), and kilometers (kilómetros), while English often uses inches (pulgadas), feet (pies), yards (yardas), and miles (millas). Gram (gramo), kilogram (kilogramo), and ton (tonelada) will be the units used in Spanish for weight; the English ones are ounce (onza), pound (libra), and ton (tonelada). When it comes to volume, Spanish uses milliliter (mililitro), centiliter (centilitro), and liter (litro), while English uses ounce (onza), cup (taza), quart (cuarto), and gallon (galón). Units in both systems are not directly equivalent and have to be converted from one system to another according to their particular relationship. For example, 1 pound is 454 grams, 1 inch equals 2.54 centimeters, and 1 gallon is 3.785 liters.

Royal Spanish Academy

The Real Academia Española (Royal Spanish Academy) was created in 1713 and is responsible for regulating the Spanish language. Its motto is "Limpia, fija y da esplendor" (It cleans, sets and gives splendor). The academy seeks to provide linguistic agreement and a common standard among all the Spanish-speaking regions. It has a formal procedure to incorporate new words, and it periodically publishes dictionaries and grammars. The academy has sometimes been criticized as too conservative and slow to react to change. It is located in Madrid and is affiliated with other national language academies in 21 Spanish-speaking countries. Its website is www.rae.es.

Political and economic facts about Spain today

Today, Spain is a democracy under a parliamentary constitutional monarchy with a hereditary monarchy and a bicameral parliament. It is a member of the European Union and its currency is the euro. Spain's capital is Madrid, and its population was estimated at 47 million in 2011. Other important cities in Spain include Barcelona, Bilbao, Valencia, Seville, and Zaragoza. Regarding religion, Roman Catholics continue to be the most numerous. Due to Spain's climate, rich historic and cultural quality, and geographic position, tourism has become one of the main sources of income for the country. Spain is also one of the most important developers and producers of renewable energy, in particular solar power.

Spanish cinema

The successful history of Spanish cinema started in the 1930s with Luis Buñuel, who was the first Spanish director to be recognized internationally through such films as *Belle de Jour*, *El discreto encanto de la burguesía*, and *Ese oscuro objeto del deseo*. He was associated with the surrealist movement and worked in Spain, France, Mexico, and the United States. Carlos Saura *(La Madriguera, Cría Cuervos, Sweet Hours)* was also a world-known Spanish director beginning in the 1950s. At present time, Pedro Almodóvar's works (*Mujeres al borde de un ataque de nervios*, *Todo acerca de mi madre*, *Volver*) are well known in both Europe and the Americas and have made household names of some of the actors (Antonio Banderas) and actresses (Penélope Cruz) that have worked in his films.

Zarzuela

The *zarzuela* is a particular type of performance art that mixes theater and music. In a *zarzuela* singing and speaking take turns. The *zarzuela* originated in Spain in the 17th century, and the pieces were very popular with the kings and other members of the privileged class. In Spain, its popularity started to decline with the arrival of opera. Nevertheless, *zarzuelas* kept on being popular in other countries such as Cuba. In the 19th and 20th century, they became popular again in Spain. The most famous composers of zarzuelas are Amadeo Vives, Federico Chueca, José Serrano, and Jacinto Guerrero.

Spanish architecture

Spanish architecture is varied and reflects its history. It had a significant Roman influence from when it was part of the Roman Empire. It then incorporated Arab features, especially in the area of Córdoba, under the Moors domination. Romanesque and gothic elements where later integrated. The 20th century brought Modernism to architecture, with Antoni Gaudi and Barcelona as its center. Contemporary Spanish architects are internationally recognized, among them Rafael Moneo (Cathedral of Our Lady of the Angels in Los Angeles, Wellesley College in Massachusetts, Museum of Fine Arts Audrey Jones Beck building in Houston), and Santiago Calatrava (Milwaukee Art Museum in Wisconsin, Ciutat de les Arts i les Ciències in Valencia, Spain, Turning Torso building in Malmo, Sweden)

Diego Velázquez

Diego Velázquez was a Spanish painter of the 17th century. Born in Seville, he moved to Madrid where he became the court painter for King Philip IV. He lived in Italy for a time but later returned to Madrid, where he died. He was mainly a portraitist, producing historical and cultural depictions of royalty, notables, and commoners. His most famous painting is *Las Meninas*, a baroque portrayal of the Infanta Margarita, one of the daughters of the king, surrounded by maids of honor and other members of the court. It is now at the Museo del Prado in Madrid. Impressionists and realists of the 19th century as well as modern painters such as Picasso and Dalí used his art as a model for their work.

Frida Kahlo

Frida Kahlo was a 20th-century Mexican painter. She was born and died in Mexico City. She contracted polio as a child, and throughout her life she suffered from this and other health issues, some of which were caused by a bus accident when she was a teenager. After the accident, she stopped pursuing medical studies and began her career as a painter. She married Mexican painter Diego Rivera. In her work, she used bright colors and simple and primitive forms deeply rooted in

- 41 -

Mexican and Amerindian culture. Her paintings were also influenced by Surrealism. She is known mainly for her self-portraits and other depictions of the feminine form. Julie Taymor directed the movie *Frida* in which Salma Hayek played the role of the artist.

Ernesto Sábato

Ernesto Sábato was an Argentine writer. He studied physics in his country and then attended the Sorbonne University in Paris and worked at the Curie Institute and later at MIT. After World War II he started to write and to be politically involved in the events of his country. He also started to paint. He translated some scientific books and wrote numerous essays and articles on literature, science, metaphysics, and politics. He is internationally recognized for his novels *El túnel*, *Sobre héroes y tumbas*, and *Abaddón el exterminador*. His second son Mario, a film director and screenwriter, directed the movie *El poder de las tinieblas*, which is based on the section *Informe sobre ciegos* from *Sobre héroes y tumbas*. Ernesto Sábato was almost 100 years old when he died.

Fernando Botero

Fernando Botero is a painter born in Medellín, Colombia. He was trained as a matador while in high school and later on lived for some time in Spain and France. In his figurative paintings, he uses exaggerated and disproportionate volumes, especially to depict the human figure, adding humorous details to show criticism and irony. His figures are easily recognized and his particular, unmistakable style is sometimes referred to as *Boterismo*. He continues to exhibit regularly and lives and works in New York and Paris.

Plácido Domingo

Plácido Domingo is a Spanish opera singer known as one of the three most famous tenors of Spain. He was born in Spain, but he was educated in Mexico. In the 1960s, he came back to Spain where he was a great success. He had done many operas including *Marina*, *Rigoletto*, *Lucia di Lammermoor*, *Carmen*, *Madame Butterfly*, and *Don Rodrigo*. He has also performed as a conductor. He first sang at the New York Metropolitan Opera in 1968, and has the record of being the singer that has appeared there the most times. Presently he is the director of the Los Angeles Opera.

Francisco Goya

Francisco Goya was a painter born in Spain in 1746. He went from the baroque, to the rococo, and then to the neoclassicism and expressionism. He worked in the Real Fábrica de Tapices de Madrid and was later appointed court painter. He was a great influence for modern artists as he was the first artist to paint what he wanted and not what the king or the church told him to paint. His paintings are mainly historic. His piece *El tres de mayo* shows the execution of Spanish soldiers by the French army. Among his best known works are *La maja desnuda*, *La maja vestida*, *El dos de mayo*, and the series of prints *Caprichos*.

José Clemente Orozco

José Clemente Orozco was a Mexican painter. Together with Rivera and Siqueiros, Orozco is one of the three main Mexican muralists. He did murals after the Mexican Revolution, and his work shows different aspects of the human condition. Besides the revolution, he focused on Pre-Columbian culture. He was less political than Rivera, but still political issues influenced his work. In his murals, messages of social justice for the working class and for the native Indians are found. Orozco's works can be found in Mexico City, Guadalajara, Veracruz, and New York. Among his best known pieces are *Omnisciencia*, *Luchas proletarias*, *La justicia*, *Riquezas nacionales*, *Buena vida*, and *La independencia nacional*.

Diego Rivera

Diego Rivera, a Mexican painter, is one of the most famous muralists in the world and the most famous of the three main Mexican muralists: Rivera, Orozco, and Siqueiros. He was influenced by the Italian Renaissance but also by the Russian communist movement. After the Mexican revolution, he painted several murals in Mexico City. Many of his pieces include the revalorization of the indigenous Mexican roots. They also include symbols and historical figures from the colonial period. His major works (*La creación, La leyenda de Quetzalcoatl, Historia de México: de la conquista al futuro, Sueño de una tar de dominical en la Alameda Central, La historia de la cardiología*) are in Mexico City in the Palacio de Bellas Artes, the Escuela Preparatoria Nacional, the Universidad Iberoamericana, and the Palacio Nacional. Other works can be found in New York and Detroit.

Celia Cruz

Celia Cruz was a Cuban singer known as the queen of salsa. She was also known as the *Guarachera de Cuba*. She was born in Cuba and later lived in the United States. Cruz and her music became a worldwide success. Her discography includes twenty three golden albums. She recorded with other artists such as Tito Puente, Johnny Pacheco and Ray Barretto. Celia Cruz is considered the most influential figure of the Cuban music in the 20th century. Her best known songs are *La vida es un carnaval, La negra te tiene tumbao, Rie y llora*, and *Usted abusó*.

David Alfaro Siqueiros

David Alfaro Siqueiros was a Mexican painter. He is one of the three main Mexican muralists: Orozco, Rivera, and Siqueiros. He painted murals in Mexico after the Mexican Revolution. His murals and other works are more realistic than those of Rivera and Orozco, but they also show aspects of Pre-Colombian culture and its relationship with colonial culture in Mexico. He was very influenced by politics and his works have Marxist messages. All his works are in Mexico City. Among his best known pieces are *Nueva democracia, Víctimas de la guerra, Víctimas del fascismo, El tormento de Cuauhtémoc, El entierro del obrero sacrificado, Los elementos, Los mitos*, and *El llamado de la libertad*.

Salvador Dalí

Salvador Dalí was a Spanish surrealist painter. He began his career as a cubist but soon, under the influence of other artists in Paris, became surrealist. His works can be found in museums all over the world. Among his best known pieces are *La cesta del pan, El hombre invisible, La persistencia de la memoria, Metamorfosis de Narciso, Madona de Port Lligat, Ultima cena*, and *Descubrimiento de América por Colón*. For those interested in Dalí, the Teatre-Museo Dalí is a tourist site in Figueres, Spain, where he was born, that includes some of his paintings and some works by other artists such as El Greco.

Isabel Allende

Isabel Allende is writer born in Peru. Shortly after, she moved to Chile with her family, and she considers herself Chilean. Allende mixed in her works the fantastic with the real. Her works could be classified as of the magic realism genre. Her most celebrate piece is *La casa de los espíritus*, in which she follows a Chilean family for four generations. In the novel, Allende examines sociopolitical issues in Chile in the postcolonial period. Other works from Allende are *De amor y de sombra, Eva Luna, Cuentos de Eva Luna, El plan infinito, Paula, Hija de la fortuna, La ciudad de las bestias,* and *Inés del alma mía.* She continues to write novels, and in 2009, she published *Los amigos son los amigos* and *La isla bajo el mar.*

Mario Vargas Llosa

Mario Vargas Llosa is a Peruvian writer who wrote novels and other political narrative pieces. As a genre, his work falls into realism. In his works he examines the vulgarity of the human nature. His topics are usually politic in nature. In 1990 he was a presidential candidate for Peru and in 2010, he received the Nobel Prize for Literature. His best known works are: *Los jefes, la ciudad y los perros, Conversación en la cathedral; Pantaleón y las visitadoras, Lituma en los Andes, La guerra del fin del mundo, Historia de Mayta, El hablador,* and *¿Quién mató a Palomo Montero?*

Alhambra

The Alhambra was built between the 12th and 13th century in Granada when the Moors occupied Spain. After the Spaniards recovered their land, the Catholic kings built their own palaces in the Alhambra, therefore it has both Islamic and Christian architectural elements. The Alhambra is a very large complex, with several buildings and different components, including courts, fountains, gardens, etc. It is known for its ornamentation, which is made of marble, stucco, and tile. At the present time it continues to be a very important touristic attraction, and in 1984, it was declared a UNESCO World Heritage Site.

Popol Vuh

The *Popol Vuh,* also known as *El libro del consejo,* was written in the Mayan-Quiché language and later translated to Spanish. There is a great deal of controversy regarding who wrote and who translated the book. In this work, the author compiles the Mayan myths that explain the creation of the world, the history of the Mayans, and some Mayan traditions. It is considered a very important source about the Mayan people of the Pre-Colombian period.

Pablo Picasso

Pablo Ruiz Picasso was a Spanish painter born in Málaga. He lived in Madrid, Barcelona, and Paris and is mainly known for his cubist paintings, though he also painted surrealist works. His art includes book illustrations and ceramics as well. Artists such as El Greco and Francisco Goya inspired him. Many of his work have a political inspiration. Picasso hated the fascist government of Franco, and he turned to communism. He was a prolific artist and many of his works are today in museums all around the world. His best known works include *Guernica, Dora Maar au chat,* and *Massacre en Corréo.*

Félix Lope de Vega

Félix Lope de Vega was a Spanish writer who wrote poetry, theater plays, and prose. He founded the Teatro Nacional de España, and he is known as the father of modern comedy. Important subjects of his work are national history and honor. His most famous theater pieces include *El perro del hortelano, La viuda de Valencia,* and *Fuente Ovejuna.* His works in prose include *Arcadia, El peregrino,* and *La Dorotea.* His poems include "El Isidro," "Rimas sacras," "La Filomena," and "La Circe."

Julio Cortázar

Julio Cortázar was a very important Argentine author who wrote stories, essays, and novels. He lived for a while in Europe, but returned to Argentina to study. He had great influence in the narrative art. He was a surrealist and his work deals with reality, fantasy, and the absurd. He used realistic images of the monstrous to transmit his ideas in his novels. His most famous works are *Rayuela, Final del juego, Bestiario, Las armas secretas, Todos los fuegos el fuego, Alguien que anda por ahí, Los premios,* and *Nicaragua tan violentamente dulce.*

Horacio Quiroga

Horacio Quiroga was a Uruguayan writer, best known for his short stories. He lived most of his life in Argentina, and he also wrote poetry. Horacio Quiroga was influenced by Edgar Allan Poe, and his stories have elements of horror, American nature, and the supernatural. He is known as a writer of the bizarre. His main work of poetry is "Arrecifes de coral." His stories include *El crimen del otro, Historia de un amor turbio, Cuentos de amor, de locura y de muerte, Cuentos de la selva, Anaconda,* and *Los desterrados.* He also wrote a short novel, *Pasado amor.*

Juan Rulfo

Juan Rulfo was a Mexican writer who wrote novels and short stories. He is considered the most profound of the Mexican prose writers of the 40s. Rulfo is known as a writer of magical realism. He created historical stories based on ignorant, poor, and desolated country people. His work deals with social injustice, hard life, pain, and suffering. The magical aspects of his works include the fantastic and the supernatural, such as the use of ghosts as characters in his works. Although Rulfo wrote only two pieces, a collection of stories, *El llano en llamas*, and a novel, *Pedro Páramo*, he won several awards.

Jorge Luis Borges

Jorge Luis Borges is one of the best known Spanish-language writers. He was born in Argentina but lived in Europe for some time. Besides writing poetry, essays, and stories, he was a professor of English literature at the Universidad de Buenos Aires. Borges founded a literary movement called *Ultraismo.* His works are fantastical and deal with metaphysical problems. Borges' genre is known as cosmovision. His most famous works of poetry are *Fervor de Buenos Aires, Luna de enfrente,* and *Cuaderno de San Martín.* His best known short stories include "Historia universal de la infamia," "El jardín de los senderos que se bifurcan," "Ficciones," "El Aleph," and "Historia de la eternidad."

Gabriel García Márquez

Gabriel García Márquez was a Colombian writer who is mostly known for his novel *Cien años de soledad.* His writing incorporates magical realism and seeks to examine the relationships between space and time and also expose Colombian life and the relationship between the social and the political in everyday life. In 1982, García Márquez won the Nobel Prize for Literature. Other novels include *La hojarasca, El coronel no tiene quien le escriba, El amor en el tiempo de cólera, El general en su laberinto,* and *Del amor y otros demonios.*

Carlos Fuentes

Carlos Fuentes was a Mexican writer, known mainly for his novels. In his novels, he examines Mexican culture and seeks a way to preserve it. His novels include universal themes and aspects of human psychology. They are based in the historical and explore real themes but in fictional works.

His novels include *La region más transparente, Las buenas conciencias, Cambio de piel, La muerte de Artemio Cruz, Aura, Zona sagrada, Terra nostra, Cumpleaños, La cabeza de hidra, Gringo viejo, Cristóbal Nonato,* and *La frontera de cristal*. His writing also includes essays and theater plays, but his novels are his most significant works.

José Enrique Rodó

José Enrique Rodó was a Uruguayan writer who wrote modernistic essays. He is known as the best modernist prose writer. His message always included a warning about the North American influence in Latin America. He wanted the Latin American youth to reject materialism and to embrace their own culture. He tried to connect modern literature with spiritualism. His best known work is *Ariel*, which has been taken as the intellectual guide for people of his generation. His work deals with democracy, morality, and idealism. Another important work of his is *Los motivos de Proteo*.

Domingo Faustino Sarmiento

Domingo Faustino Sarmiento was an Argentinian writer and politician who wrote essays and novels. He was president of Argentina from 1868 to 1874. He was also interested in education and worked as a teacher. One of his main interests was to fight against ignorance, chieftains, and dictatorship. In 1845, he wrote his novel *Civilización y barbarie: Vida de Juan Facundo Quiroga*, also known as *Facundo*. Other works by Sarmiento include *De la educación popular, Las ciento y una, conflictos y armonías de las razas de América, Mi defensa,* and *Recuerdos de provincia*.

Rubén Darío

Rubén Darío was a writer from Nicaragua, and he is a major figure of modernism. He is best known for his poetry, in which he searched for the ideal beauty. He also wrote about social problems created by materialism. He used novel meter and rhythms that transformed poetry. His most popular works are *Prosas profundas, Cantos de vida y esperanza,* and *Canto errante*. He also wrote prose, and his best known works are *Azul, Peregrinaciones,* and *Historia de mis libros*.

José Martí

José Martí was a Cuban writer and politician who is known as one of the most important writers of his times. He wrote modernistic pieces. He was a hero of the Cuban independence and fought against the Spaniards. The main message of his work is freedom and liberalism. His most important works are *Ismalillo, Versos libres, and Versos sencillos*. His most famous novel is *Amistad funesta*. He also wrote articles such as "Nuestra América," "El Presidio en Cuba," "La República Española ante la revolución cubana," and "Bases del partido revolucionario cubano." His theater play *Cartas de Nueva York* is also very well known.

Octavio Paz

Octavio Paz was a Mexican poet and essayist. He won the Nobel Prize for Literature in 1990. He can be classified neither as an idealist nor as a symbolist because his way of writing was very unique. The concepts he most often touched in his works are loneliness and existential restlessness. His most important poetry works are *Libertad bajo palabra, Piedra de sol, Salamandra, Ladera este, Topoemas, Prueba del nueve, Arbol adentro,* and *Obra poética*. The most famous of his prose work is *El laberinto de la soledad, El arco y la lira, Corriente alterna,* and *Sor Juana Inés de la Cruz o las trampas de la fe*.

Pablo Neruda

Pablo Neruda was a Chilean poet with Marxist convictions. He identified with the victims of wars, social injustice, and tyranny. He is known as one of the most important poets of the 20th century. His works are modernistic and celebrate nature and the American man. In 1971, Neruda won the Nobel Prize for Literature for his poetry, which includes *Crepúsculo, Veinte poemas de amor y una canción deseperada, España en el corazón, Residencia en al tierra, Canto general, Odas elementales,* and *Cantos ceremoniales.*

José de San Martín

José de San Martín was an Argentinian general, known as the liberator of Argentina and Chile. He fought with the Spaniards against the French in Spain's war of independence, but later he fought against the Spaniards for the independence of Latin American countries. With the help of the Chilean General Bernardo de O'Higgins, he organized the army of the Andes. San Martín unified several independence movements and helped Argentina, Chile, and Peru gain their independence. He is also known as the protector of Peru.

Cristóbal Colón

Cristóbal Colón was a Genoese navigator who sailed to the West to find a route to the East under the approval of the Catholic Kings of Spain. He won the trust of the Catholic Kings after asking the King of Portugal's approval first, but the King of Portugal had denied Colón the terms he wanted. He had three ships, the Pinta, the Niña, and the Santa María. He arrived at the new world in October of 1492. He is considered the first of the European "discoverers" of America, though he died without knowing he had not landed in the East Indies. He made several trips to the Americas, but he was never credited for his work until after his death.

Miguel Hidalgo y Costilla

Miguel Hidalgo y Costilla, better known as Miguel Hidalgo, was a Mexican priest and patriot. He is known as the father of the country, as the initiator of the independence, and as Father Hidalgo. On September 16, 1810, he gave a cry in Dolores Hidalgo, Guanajuato, known as "the cry of Dolores" that started the Mexican war of independence from Spain. He is an important figure in Mexican history, because he also ended slavery and fought for the rights of the indigenous peoples of Mexico. He succeeded in establishing a national government but soon after the Realists executed him.

Simón Bolívar

Simón Bolívar is known as the liberator of Venezuela. He also helped Peru and the Alto Peru (today's Bolivia) to obtain their independence. It is said he was the most important man of the wars for independence in South America. Besides being a general, he was an educated man and a writer. He had studied with Andrés Bello and Simón Rodríguez, who taught him the ideas of freedom. He wrote several works, including *Memoria dirigida a los ciudadanos de Nueva Granada por un caraqueño* (1812) and *Carta a Jamaica* (1815). He also wrote the constitution for the Republic of Bolivia.

Sor Juana Inés de la Cruz

Sor Juana Inés de la Cruz is known as the most important American author of lyric poetry. She lived in Mexico and wrote poetry, theater plays, and prose. Many of her works are about the disadvantages of being a woman. She was a nun, and she used solitude to escape and hide from the world and from love. She is an important representative of the baroque, and her best known works are *Respuesta a Sor Filotea de al Cruz* (prose), *Primer sueño* (poetry), and *El divino Narciso, El cetro de José,* and *El mártir de Sacramento* (theater).

Hernán Cortés

Hernán Cortés was a very successful Spanish conquistador who founded La Española in his first trip to the new world (today's Dominican Republic and Haiti). Later, he conquered Cuba and arrived in Mexico. He is known as the conqueror of the Aztecs. He took advantage of the indigenous people, and he used his alliance with the Tlaxcaltecs, enemies of the Aztecs, to defeat the Aztec empire. He was governor and General Captain of Nueva Española, and he was responsible for the abuse of other native people in the north of the country.

Aztecs

The Aztecs were an Indian group that inhabited what is now central Mexico. Before the arrival of Cortés, the Aztecs were the most powerful group in Mesoamerica. The name Aztecs covers two groups, the Aztecs and the Mexicas. The best known Aztec leaders were Montezuma I and Montezuma II. The capital of the empire was Tenochtitlan. The Aztecs had a very developed society, with different classes. They believe the daily sacrifice of a human heart was the only way to please the sun and make sure it would shine every day so they could survive. The main gods were *Quetzalcoatl*, the god of life, Tezcatlipoca, the god of the sorcerers and the young warriors, Huitzilopochtli, the god of war and the sun, Tlalok, god of the rain, and Coatlicue, the mother goddess. Their language was Náhuatl.

Mayans

The Mayans were one of the three most important indigenous groups of the Pre-Colombian world. They inhabited what today is the Yucatán in Mexico, Guatemala, Honduras, and Belize. The Mayan culture was one the most advanced in the Pre-Colombian world. The Mayans were intellectuals, and they had an arithmetic system, a calendar, and hieroglyphic writing. The *Popol Vuh* is a Mayan literary work. The best known historic Mayan sites are Palenque, Copán, Tikal, Uxmal, and Chichen Itzá. The Mayan practiced human sacrifices to appease their gods: Itzamná, the supreme god, Kinich Ahau, the sun, Txchil, the moon, and Chac, the rain. Their language was Mayan.

Incas

The Incas were the people that inhabited the region that is now Ecuador, Peru, Bolivia, Argentina, and Chile. The Incas had a very advanced culture; its social structure was based in *ayllu*, or clans. The culture was also based in communal agriculture. The Incas extended their empire over other weaker or less advanced neighboring tribes. They had a tyrannical policy and used violence to control their subjects. The most famous Inca sites are Machu Picchu, Cuzco, and Pisac. Their main gods were Inti, the sun god, and Viracocha, the supreme god. They were not as advanced as the Mayan and the Aztecs in questions of art. Architecture was their most important form of art. Their language was Quechua, which is still spoken in some parts of Peru, Bolivia, and Ecuador. The Incas practiced human sacrifices and would sacrifice a child or a virgin to please their gods. Their offerings were based on the agricultural cycle.

Colombia

Colombia is in South America, south of the Isthmus of Panama, and is the northernmost country of South America. It borders Venezuela and the Atlantic Ocean on the east, the Pacific Ocean on the northeast, Ecuador and Peru on the southwest, and Brazil on the southeast. The Andes mountains run through the country. In Pre-Colombian times, the Chibchas, the Muiscas, and the Quechuas inhabited the area. In 1501, Rodrigo de Bastidas was the first Europoean to arrive to the region. Between 1524 and 1534, the Spaniards colonized the area and called it Nueva Granada. In 1821, after many battles and changes in government, Colombia, together with Ecuador and Venezuela, was organized under the name República de la Gran Colombia. In 1830, and with the secession of Ecuador and Venezuela, Colombia ended with the same borders it has now. The Colombian economy is based on agriculture and its most important exports are coffee, corn, rice, sugar, cotton, and bananas. The capital is Santa Fe de Bogotá, and the currency is the Colombian peso.

Ecuador

Ecuador is in South America, to the south of Colombia and to the east of Peru. The Pacific Ocean is to its west. In Pre-Colombian times, several Indian tribes inhabited the area but were eventually conquered by the Incas. The center of the Incan empire was in what is today the city of Quito. In 1527, Spaniards arrived in Ecuador, and in 1533 it was conquered by Sebastián de Belalcázar. In 1563, the Audiencia of Quito was founded, but in the 17th century the area was incorporated to the Viceroyalty of Nueva Granada. After several battles and changes in government during the 18th and 19th century, Ecuador declared its independence from Spain. The economy of Ecuador is based on agriculture and the country is the largest exporter of bananas. Oil and its products are also important for the economy of Ecuador. The capital of the country is Quito, and the currency is currently the US dollar.

Venezuela

Venezuela is in South America, north of Brazil and east of Colombia. Guyana is to its east and the Caribbean Sea and the Atlantic Ocean are to its north. The Arawaks and the Caribes inhabited the area in Pre-Colombian times. The first Europeans to arrive in Venezuela were in an expedition of Alonso the Ojeda and Pedro Alonso Niño. Caracas was founded in 1567, and the area became important due to its exports of cocoa. It was part of the Viceroyalty of Nueva Granada, and the Audiencia de Caracas was formed in 1786. In 1811 it declared its independence. The economy of Venezuela is based on oil and its products. The capital is Caracas, and the currency is the bolivar.

Uruguay

Uruguay is in South America between Argentina and Brazil, in the area of the Río de la Plata. In Pre-Colombian times, several indigenous peoples inhabited the area, most notably the Charrúas, who rebelled against the Spaniards who wanted to conquer the region. In 1516, Juan Díaz de Solís arrived at the Río de la Plata, and shortly after the area we know today as Uruguay was explored. Sebastián Gaboto founded the first settlement in 1527, but it was destroyed by the Indians. In 1680, the Portuguese founded a colony that was given to the Spaniards in 1777. Montevideo was occupied by the British in 1806. After fighting against the Spaniards and the Portuguese and after several different changes in government, Uruguay was established as a state in 1825. The capital is Montevideo, and the currency is the Uruguayan peso.

Argentina

Argentina is in South America to the south of Bolivia, Paraguay, Uruguay, and part of Brazil. Chile is to its west. Several indigenous peoples inhabited the large territory in Pre-Colombian times, including the Tehuelche and Mapuche. In 1516, Juan Díaz de Solís was the first European to arrive at the Río de la Plata, and in 1536 Pedro de Mendoza founded Buenos Aires. The region was not very important to Nueva España until 1776 when Spain established the Viceroyalty of the Río de la

Plata. Argentina stayed under the dominance of Spain until 1816 when it declared its independence. Part of the Andes run through Argentina. The economy of Argentina is based on livestock and oil. The capital is Buenos Aires, and the currency is the Argentine peso.

Bolivia

Bolivia is in South America to the south of Brazil and Peru, to the east of Chile, and to the north of Argentina and Paraguay. It is interesting to note that the country does not have access to the ocean. In Pre-Colombian times, the Pukina and the Aymara inhabited the area but were under the Inca Empire. In 1530, Gonzalo and Hernando Pizarro were the first Europeans to arrive in Bolivia while they were exploring what is now Peru. Bolivia was important during the colonial period because of its silver mines in Cerro Rico in Potosí. Bolivia was part of the Alto Peru until 1776 when it was incorporated to the Viceroyalty of the Río de la Plata. In 1825, Simón Bolívar declared the independence of Bolivia. The administrative capital and seat of the government is La Paz. The constitutional capital is Sucre. It has three official languages: Spanish, Quechua, and Aymara. Bolivia's currency is the boliviano.

Paraguay

Paraguay is in South America to the south of Bolivia and to the east of Argentina. The river Paraguay divides the country into east and west. It is interesting to note that the country does not have access to the ocean. In Pre-Colombian times, the Chané, the Agacé, and, most important, the Guaraní inhabited the area. In 1524, Alejo García was the first European to arrive in the region, and in 1525, Pedro de Mendoza began colonization. Between 1735 and 1756 the Guaraní rebelled against the Spaniards. In 1777, it was incorporated to the Viceroyalty of the Río de la Plata. Paraguay fought against Spain and against Argentina, and, in 1830, declared its independence. Paraguay has two official languages: Spanish and Guaraní. The capital is Asunción, and the currency is the guaraní.

Peru

Peru is in South America to the south of Colombia and Ecuador, the west of Brazil and Bolivia, and to the north of Chile. The Pacific Ocean is at its west. The Andes mountains run through the country. Machu Picchu is located in Peru. In Pre-Colombian times, several indigenous groups inhabited the area under the Inca Empire. In 1524, Francisco Pizarro arrived to the area. Between 1531 and 1535, the region was conquered by Pizarro. In 1544, the first Viceroyalty of Peru was established. In 1572, the Inca Túpac Amaru rebelled against the Spaniards. In 1820, José de San Martín took control of the country and declared independence. The economy of Peru is based in agriculture. The capital is Lima, and the currency is the sol. The official languages are Spanish and Quechua.

Chile

Chile is in South America to the south of Peru, the southeast of Bolivia, and the west of Argentina. The Andes Mountains run through the country. The Atacama Desert is in the north. In Pre-Colombian times, the Incas inhabited the area. In 1513, Diego de Almagro was the first European to arrive to the territory. In 1552, Pedro de Valdivia conquered the area. In 1778, it was incorporated to the Viceroyalty of the Río de la Plata. After long fights lead by Bernardo O'Higgins and José de San Martín, Chile declared its independence from Spain in 1818. The economy of Chile is based in agriculture. Vinyards and exports of wine are important to the country's economy. Due to the different climates in Chile, tourism is also important. The capital is Santiago, and the currency is the Chilean peso.

Antilles

The Antilles is the archipelago in the Caribbean Sea between North and South America. The Greater Antilles are Cuba, Hispaniola (Dominican Republic and Haiti), Jamaica, and Puerto Rico. The Lesser Antilles are the islands on the east of the Caribbean Sea and include Guadeloupe, Dominica, Martinique, Saint Lucia, Barbados, Granada, Trinidad, and others. In Pre-Colombian times, they were inhabited by the Arawak and the Caribe, and it was the first land Colón put his foot on in 1492. Later, sugar production flourished and, with it, slavery. There is a large mix of races in the islands, and, due to the big imports of slaves, the influence of Africa is notable.

Panama

Panama is the farthest south of the countries of Central America and is to the north of Colombia. In Pre-Colombian times, it was inhabited by the Chocó, the Chibcha, and the Caribe. In 1501, Rodrigo de Bastidas y Colón was the first European to arrive in Panama. From 1513 to 1535, it was known as Castilla de Oro or Tierra Firme; later it was incorporated to the Viceroyalty of Peru and Nueva Granada. In 1821, it became part of Colombia. The Panama Canal, which was built by the United States, is very important to the region. Due to the influence of the United States, international enterprises have expanded in Panama. The capital is Ciudad de Panamá, and the currency is the balboa.

Dominican Republic

The Dominican Republic is on the island of Santo Domingo, which it shares with Haiti. The island was called Hispaniola (La Española), the name Colón used when he arrived in 1492. In Pre-Colombian times, it was inhabited by the Taino and the Arawak. In 1509, Nicolás de Ovando established a colony. Later, in 1511, the Audiencia de Santo Domingo was created. The Spaniards lost the island to the French in 1803, but recovered it in 1822. In 1844, independence was declared. The economy of the Dominican Republic is based on agriculture, mainly sugar cane. The capital is Santo Domingo, and the currency is the Dominican peso.

Cuba

Cuba is one of the islands of the Greater Antilles. It is to the south of Florida in the United States and to the west of the Bahamas. The most important indigenous groups that inhabited the island were the Taino, the Guanajatabey, and the Ciboney. In 1511, Diego Velásquez began the conquest of the island. Cuba, together with Puerto Rico, was the last Spanish colony in the new world. In 1891, Cuba was occupied by the United States. In 1952, Fulgencio Batista established a dictatorship, and in 1959, Fidel Castro took control of the country. The capital is Havana, and the currency is the Cuban peso.

South America

South America also known as Suramerica or Sudamerica includes Colombia, Venezuela, Ecuador, Guyana, Surinam, Trinidad and Tobago, Brazil, Peru, Bolivia, Paraguay, Uruguay, Chile, and Argentina. Its main rivers are the Orinoco (in Venezuela and Colombia), the Paraná (in Brazil, Paraguay, and Argentina), the Paraguay (in Brazil, Bolivia, Paraguay, and Argentina) and the Amazon, the longest in the world (in Peru, Brazil, Bolivia, Colombia, and Ecuador). The great mountain range of the Andes goes north to south and is the largest in the world. The Lake Titicaca is shared by Peru and Bolivia. Machu Picchu, the famous Inca site, is in Peru.

Puerto Rico

Puerto Rico is one of the islands of the Greater Antilles. It is southeast of the United States, and it is an unincorporated territory of the United States. In Pre-Colombian times, it was inhabited by the Taino. In 1493, in his second trip to the new world, Cristobal Colón arrived on the island for the first time. He named it San Juan Bautista. Ponce de León lead the conquest of the island, and it was under Spanish control until 1897, when it declared its autonomy from Spain. In 1898, it was occupied by the army of the United States. In 1899 Puerto Rico became part of the United States after the Peace of Paris ended the Hispanic-North American war. In 1950, it was set as an unincorporated territory of the United States. The capital is San Juan, and the currency is the US dollar.

Guatemala

Guatemala is to the South of Mexico. The Maya inhabited the area in Pre-Colombian times, and they had an important civilization in the area of Petén, in the northeast of the region. In 1524, Pedro de Alvarado began the conquest of the territory. In 1543, Guatemala already has its own government. The Audiencia de Guatemala was formed, and it had jurisdiction over all of Central America. In 1821, Guatemala declared its independence, and during the period from 1821 to 1838, it was part of the Provincias Unidas de Centroamérica. Agriculture is the most important sector of the economy of Guatemala, especially coffee, sugar cane, and bananas. The capital is Ciudad de Guatemala and the currency is the quetzal.

Central America

Central America is the region between North America and South America. It begins in the Tehuantepec Isthmus in Mexico and continues south to Panama. The Antilles, geographically, are a part of Central America. The countries in Central America are: Guatemala, Honduras, El Salvador, Nicaragua, Costa Rica, and Panama. In colonial times, this area was under the control of the Audiencia de Guatemala. For a few months, all these countries belonged to the Provincias Unidas de Centroamérica, but later, each one had its own independence and history. The Panama Canal, which connects the Atlantic with the Pacific Ocean, is very important to the region and the world.

El Salvador

El Salvador is the smallest country in Central America. It is to the south of Guatemala and the west of Honduras. In pre-Colombian times, it was inhabited by the Mayans, specifically the Pipile. In 1524, Pedro de Alvarado conquered the territory and founded San Salvador, today's capital. After being part of the Audiencia de Guatemala, it established itself on its own in 1786. In 1824, it incorporated with the Provincias Unidas de Centroamérica and, in 1841, it declared its independence. The country experienced a civil war from 1977 to 1979. A presidential regime was established in 1983. Coffee is the main agricultural product of El Salvador. The currency is the United States dollar.

Costa Rica

Costa Rica is located between Nicaragua and Panama in Central America. In Pre-Colombian times, it was the contact area between the Mesoamerican cultures of the south of Central America and those in the north of South America. In 1523 the expedition of Gil González Dávila entered Costa Rica as the first Europeans to do so. In 1523, Francisco Fernández de Córdoba began the conquest of the region. Later, it was under the control of the Audiencia de Guatemala. In 1823, Costa Rica was incorporated to the Provincias Unidas de Centroamérica. In 1848, it declared its independence. The economy of Costa Rica is based mainly on agriculture and fishing. Coffee, bananas, pineapple, and cocoa are exported. The capital is San José, and the currency is the Costa Rican colón.

Honduras

Honduras is a country in Central America between Guatemala, El Salvador, and Nicaragua. In Pre-Colombian times, it was inhabited by the Mayans. The Mayan city of Copán was in the west of Honduras. In 1497, Yánez Pinzón and Díaz de Solís were the first Europeans to arrive in Honduras. The conquest of the region was led by Gonzalez de Avila and Cristóbal de Olid. It was part of the Audiencia de Guatemala until 1786. In 1824, it incorporated into the Provincias Unidas de Centroamérica. In 1838, it seceded and became independent. Bananas are the main export of modern Honduras. Coffee, corn, and tobacco are also exported. The capital is Tegucigalpa, and the currency is the lempira.

Nicaragua

Nicaragua is to the southwest of Honduras and El Salvador. It borders with Costa Rica in the south. In Pre-Colombian times, it was inhabited by many Indian groups including the Nahuas. In 1522, Gil González Dávila discovered the territory. In 1524, Francisco Fernández de Córdoba began its conquest. In 1527, it was established under the Audiencia de Guatemala. In 1824, it integrated with the Provincias Unidas de Centroamérica. In 1838, it declared its independence, the first state to do so. Agriculture is the most important part of its economy. Nicaragua exports cotton, coffee, sugar, and bananas. The capital is Managua and the currency is the córdoba.

General Francisco Franco

In 1934, General Francisco Franco led a campaign against the Republican government and divided Spain between rightists and leftists. In 1936, the Spanish Civil war started and lasted three years. General Franco defeated the Republicans and established an absolute dictatorship. Under Franco, Spain changed significantly. Political prisoners under the Franco regime included scientists, artists, writers, teachers, and professors. His dictatorship was supported by the church and by the army. The dictatorship was defined by its oppression, lack of freedom, fidelity to the Catholic Church, and support from the Spanish financial oligarchy. Franco continued as dictator until his death in 1975.

Inquisition

The Inquisition was a court established during the reign of Fernando II of Aragon and Isabel I of Castile in 1480. The purpose of the Inquisition was to discover and punish heretics, and investigate crimes against the faith, including witchcraft, bigamy, blasphemy, and possession of forbidden books. Its main motivation was to ensure the orthodoxy of Jewish and Muslim converts to Christianity. It intensified after royal decrees in 1492 and 1501 ordering Jews and Muslims to convert to Christianity or leave the country. Inquisition courts used torture during interrogations. The Inquisition operated in Spain and also in Nueva España. The Inquisition was abolished in 1834.

Spanish Armada

The Spanish Armada was a strong fleet composed of more than 130 ships and 20,000 sailors. At its strongest, it was considered invincible. But, in 1588, when King Felipe II sent it to England to try to destroy Queen Elizabeth I of England, the fleet was defeated. The defeat of the fleet is considered the historical point when the Spanish empire began to decline. Spain would never have the same political and economic importance in Europe as before the defeat.

Spanish Civil War

The Spanish Civil War was between the Nationalists, under the control of General Franco, and the Republicans, composed of anarchists, communists, and socialists. The Civil War started in 1936 when General Francisco Franco led a campaign against the Republicans. The war divided communities, families, and friends. Both sides committed atrocities to each other. After the rebellion in Morocco, the big cities with big armies fell under the control of Franco. Franco extended its power little by little, with the help of the Nazis and the Italian fascists. Finally, the Franquists defeated the Republicans in Valencia and Madrid and the war ended on April 1, 1939. Once the war was over, Franco established his dictatorship.

Mexico

The official name of Mexico is the Estados Unidos Mexicanos. The country is in North America, and borders with the United States in the north, and Guatemala and Belize in the south. Its territory is three times the size of Texas. In Pre-Colombian times, it was inhabited by the Aztecs in the region's center, the Mayans in Yucatan in the south, and the Chimichecas in the north. After the arrival of the Spaniards, the Viceroyalty of Nueva España was established, and Hernán Cortés presided as Captain General over the territory he had conquered. In 1821, Mexico declared its independence from Spain. Agriculture, industry, mining, and tourism are strong areas of Mexican economy. The capital is the Ciudad de México or México D. F., and the currency is the Mexican peso.

Bourbons

The House of Bourbon is a European royal house that has French origins and had a significant influence in Europe. The most famous Bourbon in Spain was Carlos II of Spain who designated Felipe V (Duke of Anjou) as his successor. Carlos V became king in 1700 and started the War of Spanish Succession. Other important Bourbons in Spain were Luis I, Fernando VI, Carlos III, and Carlos IV. Many of the reforms the Bourbons implemented had a big impact in both Spain and their colonies in the New World.

Miguel de Unamuno

Miguel de Unamuno was an author from the generation of 98, a group of Spanish writers, essayists, and poets that were affected by the moral, political, and social crisis in Spain in the last decades of the 19th century. The main message of Unamuno was that Spain needed to abandon its traditions and integrate with Europe. In his best known essay, "Del sentimiento trágico de la vida," Unamuno exposed the conflict between reason and faith. His best known novels are *Paz en la guerra, Niebla, Abel Sánchez, La tía Tula,* and *San Manuel Bueno, mártir.*

Benito Pérez Galdós

Benito Pérez Galdós was a Spanish author who wrote realist novels, dramas, and chronicles. He is best known for his historic novels in which he mixed reality with fiction. His main goal in writing was to find and analyze the origins of the Spanish revolution of the 19th century. He wrote *Episodios nacionales*, in which he exposes the intimacy of Spaniards of the 19th century taking into account national historical facts that marked the country's collective destiny. It was a time of crisis in Spain, which is reflected in his work. Among his best known works are: *Doña Perfecta, GloriaFortunata y Jacinta,* and *Misericordia.*

Reconquista

The Reconquista refers to the attempt on the part of the Spaniards to recover their land from the control of the Muslims, who had invaded Spain in 711, and to restore a united faith (Christianity, specifically Catholicism). The process took from 712 to 1492. Almost immediately after the invasion, the Spaniards began the process of reconquering the country. In the 720s, the Christians recovered Asturias. The city of Granada was the last to be reconquered by the Spaniards.

Emilia Pardo Bazán

Emilia Pardo Bazán, also known as the Countess, was very important novelist from the last decades of the 19th century. She tried to introduce naturalism in Spain. Emilia Pardo Bazán wrote stories, novels, and poetry. She also wrote social studies and commentaries that were published in periodicals such as *El imparcial* and *La ilustración artística*. Most of her works deal with the life and customs of Galicia; the author uses her characters and situations to study the human condition. She wrote more than 500 pieces, the best known are *Los pasos de Ulloa, La madre naturaleza, Cuentos de la tierra,* and *La tribuna.*

Federico García Lorca

Federico García Lorca wrote dramatic pieces, poetry, and theater. He was a super-realist. In his works, García Lorca always offers a separate world with creations that oscillate between reality and fantasy. Among his dramas are: *Bodas de sangre, Yerma, and La casa de Bernarda Alba*. His poetry includes: *Libro de poemas, Canciones, Romancero gitano, Poema del cante jondo,* and *Poeta en Nueva York*. He lived for a while in New York and studied English at the Columbia University. He returned to Spain in 1930. In 1936, García Lorca was assassinated a few days after the Spanish Civil War started.

Miguel de Cervantes Saavedra

Miguel de Cervantes Saavedra wrote the most popular Spanish novel, *Don Quijote de la Mancha,* which was published in two parts, the first one in 1605 and the second one in 1615. In *Don Quijote de la Mancha*, Cervantes recounts the adventures of Alonso Quijano, an old man who goes crazy after reading too many chivalric novels. In his altered state, he believes he is Don Quijote de la Mancha, a traveling knight. Cervantes narrates Don Quijote's adventures and his search for love. The most famous scene is when Alonso, believing they are giants, fights against windmills. The book is considered a parody of the chivalric books of the times. Besides *Don Quijote de la Mancha*, Cervantes wrote *La galatea, Novelas Ejemplares,* and *Los trabajos de Persiles Sigismundo*, but those works were never as popular as *Don Quijote.*

The Muslims in Spain

In 711, the Muslims from the north of Africa invaded the Iberian Peninsula and conquered most of it. What is known today as Spain was under Arab control until 1492. Due to the many years the region was under control of the Muslims, Arab influence can be seen everywhere. Many of the Spanish words that begin with al- have Arab roots: *álgebra, aldea, alguacil, alférez, alcoba, algodón,* and *alcachofa*. Another example is the word *ojalá*, which comes from the phrase "may Allah grant." Many cities in Spain show buildings with clear Muslin influence. The most famous of those buildings is the mosque of Córdoba, whose architecture and tile decor is typically Arab.

El cantar del mio Cid

El cantar del mio Cid was anonymously written in about 1140. It is in the style of a singing poem, a very popular literary form in medieval Spain. *El cantar del mio Cid* takes place during the Reconquista, when the Spaniards were trying to regain control of their land from the Arabs that had been in the country since 711. The main character is Rodrigo Díaz de Vivar, who is seeking to recover his honor after being exiled by king Alfonso VI. He takes part in the battle of Valencia and, after recovering his honor, his two daughters marry the heirs of the house of Carrión, relatives of the King. These men mistreat the girls and almost kill them. The Cid fights against the bad husbands and, after defeating them, the daughters marry the heirs of the house of Navarra and Aragón. Because of this, the Cid is known as the man who unified Spain during the Reconquista.

El libro del buen amor

El libro del buen amor was written in the 1320s by Juan Ruíz. It is an interesting work because it includes different genres: narrative, lyric, and didactic. Scholars consider it a commentary on love and its behaviors. The main character, the Archpriest of Hita, presents the topic in an almost biographical way and talks about his sexual frustrations. It debates about love and if man should put aside his thirst for sex and embrace divine love instead.

Alfonso X

Alfonso X or Alfonso el Sabio (the Wise) was king of Castilla-León from 1252 to 1284. Alfonso X is important in history because of his decision of using Castilian as the official language of his kingdom. Castilian or Spanish became more important than other languages or dialects spoken in the territory. During his reign, many works were written, revealing much about medieval Spain. *The Crónica general de España* is one of these works and is very useful in understanding Spanish history.

La Celestina

La Celestina, also known as *Tragicomedia de Calisto y Melibea*, was written by Fernando de Rojas in 1499. Many considered *La Celestina* the first Spanish novel although it is not strictly a novel as it is written as a dialogue between the characters. The piece has 21 acts. It deals with the seduction of a young virgin, Melibea, and how an old woman, Celestina, tries to arrange this seduction for Calisto, the man who loves Melibea. The work begins in an orchard where Calisto meets Melibea and falls madly in love with her. Melibea does not feel the same for Calisto. Calisto goes to Celestina for help. After being together for some time, Melibea and Calisto fall in love and Celestina's help is not needed anymore, which causes a lot of trouble. By the end of the work, almost all the characters have died. Other characters in the piece are Sempronio, Elicia, Pármeno, and Pleberio.

Spain

Spain is in the Iberian Peninsula and has 50 provinces. Its five main rivers are the Ebro, the Duero, the Tajo, the Guadiana, and the Guadalquivir. Spanish is the official language of the country, although in some parts of the country other languages are spoken, for example Catalan in Catalonia, Galician in Galicia, and Basque in the Basque Country. Spain can be divided in the following regions: north, center, south, east, and extraterritorial possessions. Spain is significant as the country where the Spanish language originated. Its capital is Madrid and its currency is the euro.

Spanish territories

Three groups of islands belong to Spain: the Balearic Islands, the Canary Islands, and Melilla and Ceuta. The Balearic Islands are in the Mediterranean Sea, and include Mallorca, Menorca, and Ibiza. The capital is Palma de Mallorca. The Canary Islands are in the Atlantic Ocean, and include Santa Cruz de Tenerife and Las Palmas. Their capitals have the same name as the islands. Melilla and Ceuta are north of Morocco, and they are much less significant than the Balearic and Canary Islands.

Language Acquisition, Instruction, and Assessment

Generalizations about language education that have emerged through research

Research findings from various world educational settings indicate that academic/school language differs markedly from home language everywhere. In all settings, developing cognitive-academic language takes considerable time, i.e. 4-7 years of formal instruction. Students in all places learn cognitive and literacy skills and master academic content subject matter most easily when these are taught in languages familiar to the students. Once students have developed cognitive-academic linguistic skills, these skills easily transfer to other languages, as does their knowledge of school content subjects. Among all predictive factors, the relative degree of cognitive-academic language proficiency that a student develops in a second language is predicted <u>best</u> by that student's level of cognitive-academic language proficiency in his or her first language. An additional universal generalization found is that depending on their cultures, social groups, and individual personalities, children learn second languages in different ways. These findings support additive bilingualism, wherein instruction includes languages familiar to students.

Theories of language acquisition

Interactionist

Jerome Bruner was the main proponent of Interactionist theory, which says that interactions between the child and parents/caregivers determine the course of language development.

Nativist

Noam Chomsky is the major proponent of the Nativist or Innate theory of language development. He maintains that humans possess an internal Language Acquisition Device, allowing them to generate linguistic structures more easily and naturally than they could without it. Furthermore, Chomsky asserts that environmental factors influence, but do not determine, this process.

Cognitive

Jean Piaget was the major proponent of the Cognitive theory of language development. He viewed language acquisition as one component of a child's overall cognitive development; hence, he believed language develops following the same stages he proposed for all intellectual progress.

Behaviorist

B. F. Skinner was the major proponent of the Behaviorist view of language acquisition, which holds that children develop language the same way that all organisms learn everything. Their early linguistic responses to environmental stimuli are reinforced selectively by adults; they will repeat rewarded responses, while ignored responses are less likely to persist.

Piaget's Cognitive Developmental theory

Piaget viewed language acquisition as part of a child's overall cognitive development; therefore, according to Piaget, language acquisition follows the stages of intellectual development he proposed. Piaget stated that to acquire any specific linguistic form, a child first must be able to understand its underlying concept. Piaget defined the stages of cognitive development as Sensorimotor, Preoperational, Concrete Operations, and Formal Operations. Children in Sensorimotor and Preoperational stages cannot perceive others' viewpoints; Piaget dubbed them egocentric. Sensorimotor infants first perform reflexive activities, and then learn to coordinate their sensations and motor movements. As they become aware of objects, infants develop object-orientation and object permanence (realizing objects continue to exist when out of their sight), then intentional actions. Infants develop mental constructs (schemata) representing objects. By age 2, they internalize these schemata, thereby enabling symbolic thinking—representing things/concepts with linguistic symbols, i.e. words. Concrete Operations-stage children can perform and reverse mental operations, but only regarding concrete objects. In Formal Operations they grasp and manipulate abstract concepts, including abstract word meanings (semantics) and operations (higher-order syntax, grammar, etc.).

Noam Chomsky's LAD and his Syntactic Theory

Chomsky's Language Acquisition Device (LAD) is his theoretical construct representing an innate mechanism or tool set he says all humans possess for learning language. He finds that in all languages, the Universal Grammar (UG) rules are the same. Therefore, he has stated that "all children share the same internal constraints which characterize narrowly the grammar they are going to construct" (1977). Chomsky asserts that since the brain is part of the body, the mental world is part of the biological world in which we live. As a result, the mental world follows biological processes. He designates language development as "language growth" in that the "language organ" grows in the brain like any other bodily organ. His Syntactic Theory explains that speakers understand internal sentence structure (syntax) via "phrase structure rules." His "poverty of stimulus" argument is that children hear many fragmented/ungrammatical/unstructured adult utterances, yet still construct correct grammars, which he views as evidence of universal, inborn language abilities. He also points out that children having different experiences still form the same linguistic rules.

Skinner's Behaviorist theory explains the process of language development

According to Skinner's theory of Operant Conditioning, learning is a function of change that occurs in an organism's observable behaviors. Behaviorists see language development as a process of building behaviors through conditioning that occurs through interactions with the environment. Skinner stated that adults selectively reinforce young children's vocalizations which to them resemble recognizable speech and disregard those vocalizations they find irrelevant. Children will repeat reinforced, i.e. rewarded, responses. The child's responses gradually become more similar to adult speech through what Skinner called successive approximations. Skinner believed children acquire verbal behavior matching that of their "given verbal community" via this process. As their vocalizations approach recognized speech forms, these "produce appropriate consequences" for the children. Main principles include that positively reinforced (rewarded) behavior recurs, that responses can be shaped through presenting information in small increments, and that reinforcement promotes response generalization to other similar stimuli. Limitations include that the rules and structure of language cannot be derived through sheer imitation, and that children often cannot repeat adult utterances.

Chomsky's theory of Innate language development

Chomsky proposed the "Innateness Hypothesis" that all humans have an inborn ability to develop language, in the form of what he called "Universal Grammar" (UG) or "Generative Grammar"—a set of linguistic rules with which our brains are pre-programmed. Chomsky says that this inherent blueprint or template for language structures explains why even deaf and/or blind children and/or children with deaf and/or blind parents develop language in the same ways, following the same stages, as do all other children. Chomsky has stated that language development is an inevitable occurrence with children rather than a voluntary action. In other words, given a suitable environment, including "appropriate nutrition and environmental stimulation," they will acquire language naturally, similarly to their predetermined physical maturation processes. Chomsky's UG does not contain specific rules of every language. Instead, Chomsky's view asserts that general "principles and parameters" from which language rules are derived.

Chomsky's Transformational Grammar

Noam Chomsky has proposed that language consists of "deep structures" and "surface structures." Deep structures are the forms in which linguistic concepts originate. He says our minds then perform "transformations" which change these deep structures to surface structures, which are the final forms of our spoken and written language. For example, a basic statement is a deep structure, and we transform it to make it grammatically complete. As a result, we turn the statement into a question or a negative, or both. A deep structure might convey "He is going out." Chomsky proposes that we automatically make transformations to this structure to turn it into a question: "Is he going out?" or a negative: "He is not going out;" or both: "He is not going out, is he?" So for Chomsky, the essential concept is the same, but the semantic changes, i.e. changes in meaning, and syntactic changes, i.e. changes in sentence structure that produce such variations as questions and negatives, are achieved through transformations from the same deep structure to various surface structures.

Jerome Bruner's Interactionist theory of language acquisition

Bruner emphasizes adult-child interactions as promoting children's language acquisition. Bruner sees child-directed speech (CDS), i.e. the linguistic behaviors of adults in speaking to children, as having a specialized adaptation of supporting the process of language development. Bruner termed such support "scaffolding." The concept of scaffolding—support given to young learners as needed and gradually withdrawn as they develop more autonomy—has also been applied to Lev Vygotsky's sociocultural theory of learning, especially his Zone of Proximal Development (the distance between what a learner can do on his/her own and what s/he can do with guidance), and to Stephen Krashen's theory of ESL acquisition. Whereas Chomsky has proposed a universal Language Acquisition Device (LAD) we all possess, Bruner countered this proposal with a Language Acquisition Support System (LASS), which reflects Bruner's greater emphasis on the interactions of the learning child with the family and social environment and the support they give. Chomsky's LAD reflects innate structural ability; Bruner's LASS reflects innate social ability to interpret situations/interactions.

Concept of categorization to Jerome Bruner's theory of language acquisition

Bruner believes that the ability to categorize plays a highly important role in learning. He identifies perception, i.e. our brains' awareness and interpretation of sensory stimuli, as a form of categorization; our conceptualizing, i.e. formulating ideas, as a type of categorization; our actual learning as a process of forming categories; and our decision-making as also a kind of categorizing process. A key similarity between the theories of Piaget and Bruner is their shared belief that children have intrinsic abilities helping them to understand the world, and that their actively interacting with the environment promotes their cognitive development. A key difference between Piaget and Bruner is that Piaget focused on only the cognitive aspects of development and on the learner's interactions with/actions upon the environment, while Bruner focused more on the social aspects of learning and on the learner's interactions with parents and others. Among those social aspects is language, which Bruner stressed is important to cognitive development and represents one example of scaffolding or support.

Bruner's concept of narrative constructivism

Bruner pointed out that children learn language within the social context of communication with their parents and other people. As children grow within this social setting, they need to communicate with their parents/caregivers in their environment. Bruner said that because of this necessity, children therefore imitate and gradually learn to take on the body movements and language of these adults. This necessity establishes both the reason and the method for children's language learning. Another linguist, McNamara, has interpreted Bruner's theory further to explain that unlike the Language Acquisition Device (LAD), an innate mechanism for learning language posited by Nativist linguist Noam Chomsky, Bruner's Language Acquisition Support System (LASS), an innate ability to read and interpret social situations and interactions and hence to understand language and learn it readily, enables language acquisition in children. Bruner (1991) discussed the "narrative construction of reality," writing that our constructions of our personal ideas of reality are mediated by symbol systems including language and other "cultural products" including narrative or storytelling.

Constructivism as a theory of learning

Constructivist theory understands learning as a process in which learners actively build, or construct, new concepts and ideas upon their foundations of existing knowledge. Cognitive-developmental psychologist Jean Piaget often is credited with founding constructivist learning theory, and the work of Lev Vygotsky and Jerome Bruner, who both proposed socially-oriented theories of learning, have strongly influenced social constructivism. Bruner also posited three types and stages of development in children. Enactive representation is action-based and begins in a child's first 18 months; it is similar to Piaget's Sensorimotor stage of development in that the child learns through acting physically upon objects and observing the results. Iconic representation is image-based and develops after 18 months of age; children can then learn through observing pictures and models in addition to through actions. Piaget also theorized that children learn symbolic representation around the same age. Symbolic representation involves abstract thought without needing concrete objects. While Piaget believed this ability develops in the preteen years, Bruner believes it starts around age 6-7 years.

Scaffolding

Wood, Bruner and Ross (1976) concluded from their research that parents and other adults give children "scaffolding," or the temporary support they need to promote their cognitive growth. They found that in everyday interactions involving play, in order to help children understand new concepts and perform new tasks, adults provided support structures analogous to the scaffolds temporarily erected around buildings under construction. This analogy is consistent with the constructivist theory to which Bruner subscribed, wherein we construct our realities as well as new ideas based on our knowledge. The purposes of scaffolding include making new ideas or tasks simpler and easier for children to understand, giving learning children motivation and encouragement to learn, emphasizing the most important components of a task and/or any errors they may have made in attempting it, and supplying adult models for children of the behaviors they are engaged in learning, which the children can observe and then imitate.

Linguists about learning a second language

Many linguists believe that children possess their maximal capacity to learn a second language until around the age of six years. They consider this time a "critical period" wherein children can learn up to five or six non-native languages most easily. Between the ages of six and seven years, linguistic researchers have found that children's ability to learn additional languages decreases slightly, but they are still quite able to learn other languages between the ages of seven and 11 years. Language learning ability, though somewhat less than the optimal capacity displayed during the critical period, continues to be good for children aged 12 to 17 years. Between the ages of 17 and 31 years, the ability of individuals to acquire new languages gradually diminishes further. While linguists historically have believed that adults' language-learning ability "almost ends" around age 30-31, adults still can learn new languages, albeit less naturally and with more effort than children. More recent innovations in learning techniques (e.g. Rosetta Stone) facilitate adult language learning.

Fundamental Difference Hypothesis about learning a second language vs. learning one's first/native language

The Fundamental Difference Hypothesis states that learning a second language (L2) is different from learning a first language (L1). When babies first start to babble, they have been observed to be able to make the wide range of speech sounds found in all languages. For example, English-speaking babies may roll their /r/s as in Spanish. However, as adults selectively reinforce the vocalizations that sound like English words and those vocalizations become more like adult speech, children learning to speak English as their L1 lose this flexibility. For example, many adults and older children are no longer able to produce the rolled /r/ sound when they try to learn Spanish. Linguists hypothesize that acquisition of their L1 occupies the majority of children's linguistic faculties, reducing their openness to receiving and acquiring the features of different languages (L2, L3, L4, etc.). Another basic difference is that while learning any L1 is largely natural, even unconscious at times, learning any L2 requires more mental capacity, conscious attention, memory, effort, and even studying.

Abilities of adults and older children to learn a second language (L2) and the results

Whereas typical children learn their native/first language (L1) easily and naturally, this is not the case for adults and older children learning a second language (L2), which requires the flexibility to learn linguistic features and patterns (phonological, morphological, grammatical, syntactic, and semantic) that differ from their L1. The abilities of adults to learn an L2 includes a broad range: some adults are quite gifted at learning new languages, others are average at learning them, and others have such difficulty in trying to learn an L2 that they completely fail at it. Unlike childhood L1 development, later L2 acquisition involves many more factors. Individuals who have grown up bilingual or multilingual find it easier to learn additional languages. Motivation is a significant factor: individuals with a greater need and/or desire to learn and use another language are more successful. The quantity and quality of linguistic input they receive and output they produce are also learning factors. Another is the individual's "sociolinguistic competence," which includes communicative, strategic, and grammatical competencies.

Interlanguage and fossilization in L2 learning

When students are learning a new, non-native language, some of the rules in their first and second languages will be the same or similar, while other rules will be markedly different. For example, the syntactic (sentence structure and word order) rules of German differ so much from those of English that sentences with the same meanings would have very different word orders in each language; but because English also retains parts of its Germanic origins, there are also similarities, e.g. in the morphology of many irregular verbs and in vocabulary. Because of influences from Latin and Latinate languages such as French and Spanish, although these languages differ phonologically from English, they share many cognate words, which facilitates translation and comprehension. However, when a student applies rules from another language that do not match English rules, interlanguage results: the student is speaking neither L1 nor L2/English but something in between. Some linguists/educators have found that uncorrected interlanguage features can become resistant to change and permanently entrenched in a learner's speech, which is called fossilization.

Indirect vocabulary learning

Learning of language when a child hears or sees words used in many different contexts. Indirect vocabulary learning begins at birth. A child hears conversations all around him from his immediate family, people encountered during daily activities, and the voices on radio and television. She is surrounded by words. She learns to recognize and understand those words by how they are used, who is saying them and what is going on around him when she hears them. She learns the meanings of words and adds to her vocabulary.

Examples of how a child acquires new words through indirect vocabulary learning

- Through conversations especially between and with adults. That is one of the reasons adults should be conscious of what they say and how they say it when children are around.
- When adults read to him. Readers can enhance the experience by explaining words, answering questions, and discussing what is happening in the story.
- By reading on his own. Encouraging a child to read is one of the best ways to help him expand his vocabulary and improve his comprehension.

Context clues

Learning new vocabulary is an important part of comprehending and integrating unfamiliar information. When readers encounter a new word, they can stop and find it in the dictionary or the glossary of terms but sometimes those reference tools aren't readily available or using them at the moment is impractical (e.g., during a test). Furthermore, most readers are usually not willing to take the time. Another way to determine the meaning of a word is by considering the context in which it is being used. These indirect learning hints are called context clues. They include definitions, descriptions, examples, and restatements. Because most words are learned by listening to conversations, people use this tool all the time even if they do it unconsciously. To be effective when reading, context clues must be used judiciously because the unfamiliar word may have several subtle variations, and therefore the context clues could be misinterpreted.

Integrated language study

Students need to understand that the language process is integral to learning and developing skills in all fields of study. Language is not static or one dimensional. Students need to know that language varies depending upon the audience (parents, peers, professors); has structural rules, patterns, and conventions; and changes over time with continued use. It entails speaking, listening, and writing. It requires the speaker, the listener, and the writer to respond, interpret, assess, and integrate. In today's information age, media and technology play important roles. Besides books, newspapers, radio, and television; the Internet, CDs, DVDs and personal computers also provide information. It is critical that students be taught methods to dissect and discriminate the digital data received and learn to scrutinize the sources from which it comes. The classroom should be a place where students feel safe to explore, ask questions, take risks, and develop effective listening, speaking and writing skills.

Improving students' listening and speaking skills

The most effective way a teacher can improve students' listening skills is to set a positive example by listening carefully to what each student says to him, what students say to one another, and being attentive during class discussions. Explain how to listen; for example, paraphrasing what someone said to make sure the meaning and intent is clear. Discuss why the message was clear or why it wasn't. Set up different listening situations: one-on-one, small groups, formal speeches, oral reading, student presentations, and class discussions. Rate the effectiveness of each.

One way students learn good speaking skills is by listening to good speakers so teachers should always use proper language when lecturing to the class, interacting with small groups, and during conversations with individual students. Assign a variety of speaking activities such as speeches, skits, debates, and story-telling. Have students take turns leading class discussions, reading aloud, and making formal presentations. Rate the effectiveness of each.

Improving students' reading and writing skills

A teacher can influence students' reading skills by frequently reading to the class with expression and enthusiasm, sharing her love of reading, and explaining how reading helped her in life. Assigning different genres such as novels, poetry, short stories, essays, editorials, and biographies in the target language keeps students from getting bored because they read nothing but textbooks. Allow students to decide what they want to read and lead a class discussion about the topic. Encourage critical thinking by asking probing questions and posing different scenarios.

Teachers can alleviate students' fear of writing by sharing their experiences with the writing process and reading examples of their own written work in the target language, assigning essays, reports, and term papers and giving students the tools to complete the task. Giving students the latitude to choose subjects on which to write encourages creativity. Critiquing and editing during the writing process helps the student learn to think critically and assess his own work more accurately.

Literary sociogram

A literary sociogram is a diagram of how the characters in a story are related. This graphic organizer illustrates students' understanding of and insight into the text, explores their ability to make inferences, and enhances critical thinking skills. It can be especially helpful if the story has a lot of characters, if new characters are continually added, and if the relationship between characters changes as the plot progresses. A literary sociogram can be used to define the relationship of people in an account of a real incident, such as a newspaper article, or a radio, television, or Internet news story. Characters are placed in a circle in which size indicates importance. The protagonist is placed in the center; other characters are situated according to their relationship to him and to each other; e.g., close or peripheral, friend or foe. Relationships are shown with a solid line (substantiated) or a broken line (inferred.)

Plot profile

A plot profile, or plot line, is a timeline of events and their impact upon and importance to the development of the story. The horizontal axis shows the sequence of events, while the vertical axis indicates its importance to the story. This graphic illustration helps students understand how the story is structured and enhances their analytical and critical thinking skills. The plot profile can show significant events, changes in the relationship of characters, steps the protagonist uses to resolve the conflict, or, for example, it can compare a nineteenth century novel with a contemporary television show. If there are several sub-plots, they can be added using different colors. This helps students appreciate the complexity required to create an interesting book, script, or screenplay and gives them an overview of the entire story and how all elements work together. Students should be prepared to justify their choice of events and why they believe the scenes are pivotal.

Language, vocabulary, pronunciation and grammar

The American Heritage College Dictionary defines language as "voice sounds and written symbols representing these sounds, in combinations and patterns, used to express and communicate thoughts and feelings." Vocabulary is "all the words of a language."

Vocabulary (a set of words), pronunciation (how the words are spoken) and grammar (rules governing how to use the words) are all vital elements in learning, understanding and properly using a language. If one or more elements are not learned, learned inadequately, ignored or misused, communication is impaired. The depth of a person's vocabulary and her ability to speak and write effectively is often used as a measurement of intelligence and frequently reflects the level and quality of her education.

Pronunciation is a "way of speaking a word, especially a way that is accepted and generally understood."

Grammar is the "rules of a language viewed as a mechanism for generating all sentences possible in that language."

Components of language

There are four main components of all languages: reading, writing, speaking and hearing. The following definitions are from The American Heritage College Dictionary.

- Reading is "the act or activity of rendering text aloud." To Read is "the ability to examine and grasp the meaning of written and printed material in a given language."
- Writing is "meaningful letters or characters that constitute readable material." To Write is "to form letters, words or symbols on a surface such as paper with an instrument such as a pen." (People also use typewriters and computer keyboards.)
- Speaking is being "capable of speech involving talking, expressing or telling." To Speak is "to convey thoughts, opinions or emotions orally."
- Hearing is "the sense by which sound is perceived." To Hear is "to be capable of perceiving sound by the ear."

Good reading skills

Reading is the process of understanding written information and ideas. Before the industrial revolution in the late nineteenth and early twentieth centuries, only a small percentage of the population was literate. The skill wasn't deemed necessary for most people. Preventing certain segments of the community from learning to read was also an effective way to keep them from fully participating in society.

There are several reasons for reading: memorizing, learning and comprehension, skimming, scanning and proofreading. All have their uses. Proofreading detects errors in grammar and content. Skimming and scanning are used to process large quantities of information quickly when just surface comprehension is needed. Memorizing remembers and stores information for later retrieval. Understanding and comprehension are the main reasons most people read.

Methods used to teach languages other than English

The three methods most commonly used to teach languages other than English are grammar-based, communication-based and content-based. Grammar-based methods teach students the rules of the target language including structure, function and vocabulary. Emphasis is on the why and how of the language. Communication-based methodology teaches students how to use the target language in every day, realistic situations. This approach emphasizes practical conversational usage. Content-based methodology teaches students grammar and vocabulary and uses written assignments in order to practice these skills. This approach includes using the target langugue as the main method of classroom communication between the teacher and the student and amongst students. This method emphasizes an integrated approach to learning the target language.

Continuum of learning theory

The Continuum of Learning theory outlines predictable steps when learning a new language:

- The Silent/Receptive or Preproduction stage can last from a few hours to six months. Students usually don't say much and communicate by using pictures and pointing.
- In the Early Production stage, students use one- and two-word phrases. They indicate understanding with yes or no and who/what/where questions. This stage can last six months.
- The Speech Emergence stage may last a year. Students use short sentences and begin to ask simple questions. Grammatical errors may make communication challenging.
- In the Intermediate Language Proficiency stage students begin to make complex statements, share thoughts and opinions and speak more often. This may last a year or more.
- The Advanced Learning Proficiency stage lasts five to seven years. Students have acquired a substantial vocabulary and are capable of participating fully in classroom activities and discussions.

Interpersonal communication skills

Basic interpersonal communication skills encompass two different and distinct styles of communication:

- In context-embedded communication, various visual and vocal props are available to help the student understand that which is being said, including pictures and other objects to graphically explain and communicate demonstratively. The speaker's gestures and tone of voice help the listener understand the words being used. Conversations with speakers who use hand gestures and stories with pictures and props help the learners understand more quickly and easily.
- Context-reduced communication does not have visual clues and cues and therefore the learner must rely on his competency and fluency in the language. Phone conversations, for example, do not allow the listener to see the speaker and thus hand gestures and facial expressions and other visual aides are missing. Reading a note without pictorial guides may make it difficult for the student to understand the written words.

Cognitive demands made when communicating

Depending upon with whom the conversation is had, where it is occurring and the complexity of the subject, different cognitive abilities are required of the speaker and the listener. When a student is in a relaxed, informal setting such as on the playground or in the lunchroom, the conversation between listener and speaker does not require a great deal of abstract or critical thinking. When a teacher asks a simple question requiring a yes or no answer, it is usually not threatening or stress producing. This is a cognitively undemanding communication. However, when the student is required to hear, analyze and respond quickly to abstract or complex ideas and concepts, he suddenly finds himself in a cognitively demanding communication situation. These encounters can happen during classroom discussions, when meeting new people and in unfamiliar surroundings and can pose significant challenges for learners.

Total Physical Response

Developed by James J. Asher in the 1960s, Total Physical Response (TPR) uses physical activity to reinforce the words and phrases being taught. Depending upon the age and level of language proficiency, students are given a series of simple to complex commands and/or instructions. They are expected to respond appropriately. TPR is a tool that is effective when incorporated with other methods.

Accessing Prior Knowledge

No matter what the age or level of English proficiency, students come to school with knowledge and experience. Building on and Accessing Prior Knowledge encourages them to explore new ideas and learn new concepts. A teacher who asks the student what he already knows about the subject and then lets him decide that which he wants to discover creates a positive environment in which to learn. If a student is interested in a topic, he is usually more excited about and engaged in learning more.

Technical quality of assessments

One issue that must be considered when developing academic assessments is the technical quality of the examination. The National Center for Research on Evaluation, Standards and Student Testing (CRESST) developed the following criteria to evaluate technical quality:

- Cognitive Complexity: requires problem-solving, critical thinking and reasoning ability.
- Content Quality: correct responses demonstrate knowledge of critical subject matter.
- Meaningfulness: students understand the value of the assessment and the tasks involved.
- Language Appropriateness: clear to the students and appropriate to the requested task.
- Transfer and Generalization: indicates ability to complete similar tasks and the results permit valid generalization about learning capabilities.
- Fairness: performance measurements and scoring avoid factors irrelevant to school learning.
- Reliability: consistently represents data added to students' background knowledge.
- Consequences: it results in the desired effect on students, instructors and the educational system.

Articulation matrix and Bloom's taxonomy

An articulation matrix is the relationship between activities and outcomes. It is a defined set of goals and the methods used to reach them. For example in a graduation matrix, completing the required courses is the outcome, and the lectures, homework assignments, projects, papers, tests, and evaluations are the activities.

Bloom's Taxonomy, which is a hierarchical classification system, is an articulation matrix that outlines six levels of cognitive learning. At each step, students reach a predictable level of mastery:

- Knowledge Level: ability to define terms.
- Comprehension Level: finish problems and explain answers.
- Application Level: recognizes problems and uses methods to solve them.
- Analysis Level: ability to explain why the process works.
- Synthesis Level: can use the process or part of it in new ways.
- Evaluation Level: can create different ways to solve problems and use designated criteria and can select the best method to obtain the correct solution.

Assessment station

An assessment station is a designated area, inside or outside of the classroom, used for the specific purpose of evaluating students' progress performing a task. Individuals or groups can be assigned to complete a task, use a piece of lab equipment or work with some technological device. The purpose is to assess the knowledge acquired, processes used, skills displayed, and general attitude about the task, and if working in a group, how each student interacts with the other members of the team.

The assessment station should function the same way every time it is used. This builds consistency and reduces the time needed for explanations and demonstrations before and during future assessments. Instructions should be clear, concise and specific and explain exactly how the area should be left for the next student. Activities performed in the assessment station should be simple, straightforward and relate to the material being studied.

Because the assessment station is an interactive tool, the area needs to be equipped with the appropriate equipment necessary to complete the task. The students need to understand how to operate the instruments in a safe manner and therefore instructions should be provided both in writing and verbally. Questions should be asked and answered before any activity is started. If it is a group activity, each student needs to contribute to the assigned task.

The work submitted by each student is evaluated using a rating/grading scale or a checklist. For example if the task required the use of a microscope, the checklist should have points related to its use. If it was a group project, cooperation, helpfulness and leadership skills should be noted.

Individual assessments

Individual assessments focus on the progress each student made during a defined period of time (e.g., every six weeks, at the end of the semester) rather than in a team collaboration. A variety of activities such as written assignments, oral presentations, and class participation should be incorporated into the assessment in order to obtain a broader, more realistic view of the student's understanding of the material. The assessment process should be fully explained so that the student knows what is expected. He is evaluated using one or all of the following standards:

- self-referenced —based on his previous level of progress
- criterion-referenced — a defined, school or district-wide standard
- norm-referenced — based on the progress of groups of students the same age or grade level

Using a combination of standards instead of relying on one method presents a clearer, more accurate picture of the student's growth.

Portfolio

A portfolio is a collection of the student's work assembled over a period of time (e.g., six week grading period, one semester, the entire year). Various items can be included: contracts, copies of completed activities such as papers; presentations and pictures of props; performance assessments made by the student, his peers, and the teacher; copies of class work and homework; classroom tests; and state-mandated exams. A portfolio is a powerful aide in assessing the student's progress and an excellent format to present to parents so they can review their child's progress. The decision on what to include should be a collaboration between the student and the teacher. What will be included: examples of best work, worst work, typical work, or perhaps some of each? Will the student keep a copy as a reference point? Decisions need to be made and rules established as early as possible in the process so that progress is accurately and fairly recorded.

Once decisions have been made about what will be included, it is important to begin with baseline data for comparison as the portfolio grows. Selected material can be placed in a folder or large envelope with the student's name on the front. Each addition needs to be dated with an explanation attached stating why the item was included and what features should be noted. Teachers who use portfolios will often create assignments with the intention of including it in the package. As the contents grow, it may become necessary due to space limitations to review the items and remove some daily work, quizzes, or tests. Once the portfolio is complete, the teacher needs to have a method to evaluate the contents and review the student's progress in areas such as creativity, critical thinking, originality, research skills, perseverance, responsibility, and communication effectiveness. A checklist can be useful (see card 192).

Data recording

There are three ways to record data about individual student performance. Each provides important information and lends itself to evaluating different aspects of student growth.

- Anecdotal Records are observations of day-to-day activities, e.g., how the student interacts in a group, his ability to complete a hands-on assignment, his demeanor while taking tests, and his development of particular cognitive skills. All these offer opportunities for teacher comments.
- The criteria on Observation Checklists vary depending on what the teacher wants to evaluate. They can be used to measure the growth of knowledge, a change in attitude, or the understanding of new skills. Checklists can also be used to evaluate written assignments, oral presentations, class participation, completion of individual and/or group work, or any activity that requires assessment.
- Rating Scales are similar to observation checklists. The difference between the two is that checklists are used to determine the presence or absence of a skill, while rating scales measure the quality of the performance.

Anecdotal record

An anecdotal record is a written description of observed behavior. They are usually kept in an alphabetized book, binder, or folder and should be organized so it is easy to find notes concerning a particular student. There are computer programs available that make retrieving the data simple.

To be effective, observations need to be made frequently and incidents need to be described completely and objectively; the teacher's analysis should be used as a guide for appropriate responses. Both successful situations and unsuccessful attempts need to be recorded in order to present an accurate picture of the student's progress.

The evaluation context is:

- Formative: recalling the incident may raise an alert that something that needs to be addressed.
- Summative: since observations are made over a period of time, they are an effective way to track student attitude, behavior, knowledge acquired, cognitive skills learned, etc.
- Diagnostic: consistent attention to performance may spotlight areas that need special attention.

Sample form that might be used as an anecdotal record for a group discussion

Anecdotal record for a group discussion
Subject Under Discussion: _____
Students' Names: _____
Date and Time Period of Observations: _____
Characteristics to be evaluated: _____
Balance between talking and listening: _____
Respect for others: _____
Actively participating in discussion: _____
Stating own opinion: _____
Acted as scribe: _____
Effectiveness: _____
Acted as reporter: _____
Effectiveness: _____
Acted as participant: _____
Effectiveness: _____
Acted as time-keeper: _____
Effectiveness: _____

NOTE: form may be modified to fit the observer's particular requirements.

Observation checklist

An observation checklist is a list of specific skills, behaviors, attitudes, and processes that are relevant to a student's development and contribute to his ability to successfully complete learning activities. To be effective, these checklists need to be used frequently and be collected over a period of time. One or two observations can be misleading and will not provide an accurate measurement to reach a fair evaluation. Before a using a checklist, a teacher must decide upon its purpose, how and when it will be used, and what the criteria will be. During the observation period, all occurrences of each item shown on the list need to be recorded. It is helpful for later evaluation if the teacher has a quick reference shorthand system to describe each appearance, e.g., ! equals excellent, @ equals adequate, ? equals iffy, X equals inappropriate. After the session, notes should be added to clarify or elaborate the shorthand ratings.

Developing an observation checklist takes time. It can be helpful to write down all the skills, behaviors, attitudes, and processes required to acquire mastery of the subject and that are appropriate for the particular age group. The language should be simple and easy to understand, so that the checklists can be used during student and parent conferences. Items needed for the specific task or activity to be evaluated can be chosen from the master list. There should be no more than twelve items on a checklist: any more than that becomes difficult to track, especially when observing several students at the same time. Individual checklists can be developed for specific functions, e.g., participation in a class discussion, proficiency at using a microscope, the mechanics of preparing a term paper. Whatever the rating scale, it must be used consistently, applied fairly, and easy to use during the observation period.

Observation checklist that could be used to evaluate a class discussion

Observation Checklist
Subject Being Discussed: _____
Date: _____ Class: _____
Time Elapsed: _____

	Student Names		
Spoke Clearly			
Listened to Other Opinions			
Waited for turn			
Comment was Relevant			
Challenged a Comment			
Stated Reasons for Challenge			
Noticed a Discrepancy			
Stated a Relationship Between Ideas			
Offered a Conclusion			
Inclusive Behavior Shown			

NOTE: can be modified according to teacher requirements.

Rating scale

A rating scale is used to evaluate a student against a predetermined continuum. It is particularly useful for rating an oral presentation such as a speech, debate or stage performance, and for students to use as a self-assessment tool. To increase the scale's reliability, when developing the criteria to be evaluated, the activity needs to be broken into specific, manageable parts. Each criterion may need its own rating system. Scale points need to be created.

- Will the evaluation be based upon the one to five number scale with five being the highest, or
- Will the Very Good/Good/Average/Poor/Very Poor standard be used?
- Will another system be developed?

It is helpful for the teacher to decide at the beginning of the semester which units of study will be evaluated using this method and to develop the criteria and rating system ahead of time.

Oral assessments

Oral assessments are used for two reasons: when written assessments are not feasible, and to evaluate a student's mastery of such topics as verbal language proficiency, debating skills, and the ability to think and respond quickly. These types of assessments can be stressful and some students may have trouble responding and become tongue-tied; and therefore it is important to conduct the session in private or in an atmosphere of acceptance. As an interactive form of communication, the teacher needs to avoid filling in the blanks and providing body language clues that might influence the student's response. It is also important to avoid accentuating gender, race, or cultural differences in the content or delivery of the questions and/or tasks. The examination period should be long enough and the tasks required general enough in order to ensure that the student's knowledge and proficiency can be adequately presented and evaluated.

Homework

Homework should never be assigned as punishment or due to the teacher falling behind as a result of a poorly executed lesson plan or due to outside circumstances. It should be used if students are unable to complete a project during class, to gather information, to practice new skills, or to devise a solution to a complex problem based on a real life situation. Assigned tasks should be interesting and relevant to the students' daily experiences.

Guidelines for assigning homework:

- Provide clear, unambiguous, written instructions.
- Explain what is expected and how the results will be evaluated.
- Answer questions and address concerns.
- Make sure the due date is reasonable.
- Consider other academic requirements students may have.
- Be sure resource material is adequate and readily available.
- Collect the assignment on the date specified, grade it, and return it promptly.
- Be consistent with assessment protocol and provide thoughtful, helpful comments.

Preparing tests

It is a good idea to use several types of questions when preparing tests. This will prevent the students from getting bored, expose them to a variety of testing formats, and encourage them to recall and respond to information in different ways. Matching and true/false questions are an excellent way to quickly assess how well students remember specific facts, as well as their ability to memorize data. Multiple choice and short-answer questions require a little deeper knowledge of the subject and better reasoning and thinking skills. These four testing options are reasonably quick and easy to grade. Open-response questions can be used to evaluate in depth content knowledge, the use of critical thinking skills, and the ability to communicate thoughts and ideas through the written word. This option requires more time, effort, and concentration to evaluate fairly, and is a more effective tool in some situations and courses than it is in others.

Quality tests and quizzes

Tests need to ask the right questions to accurately measure students' knowledge. There are several things to consider:

- Does each item represent an important idea or concept? If students understand the main objectives, their knowledge should be evident in their responses.
- Is each item an appropriate measure of the desired objective? Consider information presented and teaching strategies used.
- Are items presented in easily comprehensible language with clearly defined tasks? Students should not have to decode words or wonder what the item is asking them to do.
- Is the difficulty of the item appropriate? It should not be too difficult or too easy to complete.
- Is each item independent and free from overlap? Completing one item should not lead to completing additional items.
- Is the subject matter covered adequately?
- Is the test free of gender, class, and racial bias? Choose examples that are either familiar or unfamiliar to everyone.

Evaluating the effectiveness of a test

Teachers should have confidence that a test accurately measures students' knowledge: therefore it is important to monitor its effectiveness each time it is used. Before the test is given, all items should be reviewed to ensure that they still meet the criteria established for understanding the material and if one item does not meet the criteria, either rework it or remove it. If most students, including the better ones, miss the same question, perhaps it is too difficult or is not worded properly. If the item is salvageable, rework it, and if not, delete it. Asking for student feedback on one or two items is an effective way to determine if they are still appropriate or if they should be reworked or removed. Veteran teachers usually develop a "feel" for whether a test is an accurate reflection of what students know. If individual items or entire tests are reused, it is imperative to keep them in a secure place to minimize the possibility of cheating.

Effective time management ideas

Effective time management is crucial for every teacher. Accurate, fair assessment of students' academic and social progress is equally important. It is critical to develop ways to accomplish both efficiently. Organization is a key ingredient in the equation; time spent searching for things is time wasted. Collaborating with colleagues to develop assessment tools; sharing instructional methods, testing techniques, and formats that work; and establishing standards and priorities for evaluations take time in the beginning but ultimately save time. Teachers who expect perfection from themselves and/or their students are striving to reach an unrealistic goal. Using evaluation tools with appropriate frequency, assessing their value at regular intervals, constructing and saving good testing items, and using standard formats when possible are all ways to use time efficiently. Preparing lessons, organizing record keeping and evaluating the effectiveness of each on a regular basis will help develop a sensible, workable use of limited time resources.

Factors that exert negative influences on learning second or additional languages

The traditional method of teaching and learning new languages, often called the "Grammar Translation Method," has been associated through research findings with a lack of motivation and poorer results in learning new languages. These results are attributed to the inherently boring

- 73 -

quality of the method. Methods of rote memorization, drilling, and practicing "Basic Dialogue Sentences," historically used in schools often are found similarly dull and uninspiring. Educators have found that more innovative, engaging, active, and interactive teaching and learning methods can motivate students more to learn new languages, enjoy learning more, and result in better learning. Another barrier exists with language disorders. For example, the brain disorder of aphasia interferes with a person's ability to understand spoken language (Wernicke's aphasia) or to express oneself in speech (Broca's aphasia) through finding words and constructing grammatical utterances. An additional negative factor is the "affective filter," which consists of aversive feelings such as discomfort, stress, self-consciousness, and/or lack of motivation associated with L2 learning, most common in adults and older teenagers.

Applying the principles of behaviorist theory regarding language learning

In order to teach LOTE, a teacher likely would introduce lessons in the target languague and academic content subjects in small, manageable portions following the behaviorist principle of presenting new material in small amounts. This practice facilitates more precise shaping of new learned behaviors and enables LOTE students to learn more easily. The educator would demonstrate the target language in spoken and written form in order to provide a model for students to imitate, another behaviorist principle. The teacher would be sure to reward correct student responses following the behaviorist principle of positive reinforcement, thereby increasing the students' likelihood of repeating these responses. Behaviorism finds that only outwardly observable and measurable behaviors can be changed and thus disregards internal states, which it cannot observe, measure, or change. As a result, the teacher would use tests, quizzes, in-class and homework assignments, etc. and score these assessments quantitatively in order to measure correct and incorrect responses. Increases in the former and decreases in the latter would indicate learning, which behaviorism defines as observable, measurable changes in behavior over time.

Attitudes and approaches of languages other than English teachers that would reflect Chomsky's theory of language acquisition

According to Chomsky, learning language is not something that children actually do, but is a natural process occurring universally in children as they develop. Chomsky has stated that we live in a biological world; the body—including the brain, and the "language organ" he believes our brains inherently possess—physically matures over time according to predetermined patterns. Chomsky proposed that we are born with a Language Acquisition Device (LAD) in our brains, thereby facilitating language development. He allowed that children need proper nutrition and environmental stimulation in order to nurture the natural language development enabled by the LAD. Therefore, LOTE teachers would want to ensure their students receive optimal physical nourishment and stimulus-rich environments, under the teacher's influence at school and at home inasmuch as this is possible. Because Chomsky that found all humans share Universal Grammar (UG) regardless of individual languages, LOTE teachers would emphasize basic commonalities between English and the target language in order to help them relate the two languages. Differences could be addressed through correcting target languague errors over time as students' target language proficiency progresses.

Albert Bandura's Social Learning Theory

Bandura's Social Learning Theory has been viewed as building a bridge between behaviorist theories such as Skinner's and cognitive theories such as Piaget's because Bandura's theory explains human behavior through mutual interactions among environmental, behavioral, and cognitive factors. Like Bruner, Bandura emphasizes the role of social influences in learning. While behaviorists believe that the environment produces changes in behavior, Bandura believed in addition to this that behavior also produces changes in the environment. Because interactions are always two-way in Bandura's view, he called this Reciprocal Determinism. While Bandura studied social phenomena such as adolescent aggression more than language development, his theory can be applied usefully to LOTE teaching, especially in regard to modeling, imitation, and observational/vicarious learning. Conditions Bandura found required for modeling are: Attention, Retention, Reproduction, and Motivation. Imitating models is motivated not only by past events (as in behaviorism), but also by promised/anticipated rewards (internal expectations vs. behaviorism's external stimuli), and vicariously, i.e. observing another student receiving rewards for a behavior and imitating that modeled behavior to procure similar rewards.

Giving LOTE lessons more structure

Organizing what is taught and learned in LOTE classes gives students more structure, easing some of the bewilderment and challenges of learning another language. Teachers can organize their lessons according to specific topics, which they can allow the students to select. This organization has the benefit of ensuring that a topic is interesting to the students, and it affords more cohesive learning than simply teaching a number of unrelated linguistic exercises. It allows teachers to adjust for the variety of learning and proficiency levels they find among students and for the disparity of levels some individual students present among the various domains of target language and academic content performance. Organizing each lesson by limiting it to an individual topic— which can range from world peace to grocery shopping or anything in between—also allows the teacher to ensure that s/he provides each student with enough assistance focusing on the individual target language skills they need to develop, such as pronunciation, spelling, reading, writing, spoken fluency, academic content vocabulary, and etc.

Emphasizing in-depth treatment of instructional materials over a breadth of materials

Educators find that instead of using many textbooks, worksheets, etc., wearing out the copy machine and themselves, teachers can expand thoroughly on each single material. Rather than assigning many stories to read with only one accompanying activity apiece, teachers can have students read one story, discuss the story in class, discuss the story among themselves, write about the story, write about what others have said/written about the story, read what other students have written about the story, get listening practice through dictation of the story; etc. An additional benefit of this thorough treatment is that repetition is crucial to second-language learning. Another way that LOTE teachers can save time while also pursuing a topic or material in more depth involves minimizing photocopying and/or making multiple printouts. For example, rather than copying 10 different exercises from a printed resource, they can copy one exercise and then come up with 10 different activities their students can do with it. In-class dictation also eliminates copying and provides listening and writing practice.

Expanding LOTE students' vocabulary, syntactic, and grammatical learning when presenting words

Experienced teachers recommend that whenever the teacher presents a word to LOTE students, s/he should expand on it. For example, when presenting nouns, the teacher can include their plural forms, and mass nouns related to count nouns, e.g. letter, letters, mail. When presenting verbs, the teacher can include which prepositions it can take and how each preposition affects the word's meaning. Another technique involves using graphic visual reminders. Using the visual modality reinforces and supplements auditory instruction in speaking the target language.

Significance of the teacher's movements in LOTE instruction

LOTE teachers should realize that not only their words, but also their movements transmit considerable meaning. Researchers have found that in a presentation, only 10% of its impact comes from words, 30% comes from the presenter's voice, and 60% comes from movement. The definition of movement includes the teacher's appearance, facial expressions, posture, gestures, and other body language. Because verbal and analytical activities are performed in the brain's left hemisphere, many instructional activities focus on operations using the left hemisphere. However, educators advise including activities that also use the right hemisphere, e.g. music, art, creative work, visualization, imagination, dance, and other spatial and kinetic functions. Using multiple modalities strengthens learning, exercises both sides of the brain, and provides balance, variety, and enjoyment. It also affords LOTE students access to learning in the target language via avenues other than already knowing the target language. Students not only love singing, it also reinforces language sounds and intonational patterns. Teachers also can make partial/unfinished/ambiguous drawings, which students must complete and then write about them.

Incomplete stories, Bingo games, and scrambled word games can support LOTE instruction

Some teachers read obscure fairy tales or other stories to their LOTE students, omitting the ending. The students then must supply an ending, which they determine by asking questions probing for more information. One variation involves restricting questions to those with "yes/no" answers. This method enhances students' listening comprehension, spoken language skills, question construction, sense of plot structure, learning engagement, imagination, and fun. Many teachers also use Bingo to give language reinforcement and practice. With beginning LOTE students, some teachers limit Bingo letters to vowels, giving students practice in recognizing/differentiating target language vowel sounds and also the numbers used, while they have fun. Another technique involves writing a fairly long (9-10 letters) scrambled word on the board and having students, as a class or in small groups, see how many 1-letter, 2-letter, 3-letter, etc. words they can make from its letters. This method also challenges each student to unscramble the original word. This game can last from 5-45 minutes and helps build vocabulary.

Example of a game that LOTE teachers can give students that combines use of the spoken target language, listening comprehension, and drawing

Some LOTE teachers have devised games to give students practice in speaking and listening in the target language, combined with drawing. For example, two students sit back to back so they cannot see one another or the materials they hold. One student is given a picture containing abstract figures; the other is given blank paper and pencil. The student holding the picture must describe in English the sizes, locations, and shapes of the abstract forms; the other student must try to draw what the first student describes. By taking turns, each student gets practice using the target language to describe specific properties, and practice understanding the target language in speech, interpreting it, and following directions. Adding the element of drawing engages the brain's right hemisphere, balancing the left hemisphere's verbal and analytical functions, and reinforcing verbal learning and giving students another modality through which they can apprehend the target language.

Questionnaire instruments can be effective teaching tools for LOTE classes to stimulate target language expression, communication, and discussion

Scholars including those studying area linguistics, sociology, cultural anthropology, and history have long used questionnaires to collect oral history from informants. This method is invaluable for gathering information from illiterate informants. It is equally useful with literate informants for eliciting a wealth of detailed personal history. The conversational format stimulates more recollections, disclosures and expressions. These questionnaires, available from local public libraries and universities (though they may have to be translated into the target langugage), have the same effect of stimulating conversation and discussion with LOTE students. For example, they include items such as describing one's childhood home, including layout, rooms, and sleeping arrangements; how and/or which members of the family shopped, cooked, served, ate, cleaned up after meals; how they did laundry; what jobs family members had; memories of childhood experiences, e.g. times they had the most fun, the worst trouble they got into; family pets, etc. Speaking an unfamiliar, non-native language is easier for LOTE students when the subject matter is familiar and personal to them. Discovering similarities and differences with other students' backgrounds also stimulates interest and discussion.

Fundamental ways that Spanish differs from English with respect to spelling, pronunciation, and reading

In Spanish, words are spelled more phonetically much more consistently than in English. (Consider that in English rough, though, through and bough, the letter combination -ough is pronounced four different ways with the same spelling, and none of these pronunciations matches that spelling.) Because the look and sound of Spanish words correspond more, the syllable is a more important phonological awareness unit and predicts successful Spanish reading. English learning employs sight word recognition because many English words cannot be decoded for sound based on their irregular spellings (e.g. are, one or the –ough words above); Spanish does not use sight words because decoding is straightforward due to its more transparent spelling. Thus, Spanish students learn to decode faster and soon move on to comprehension and fluency. Spanish instruction employs most frequently used words rather than sight words. Comprehension is a more significant issue in Spanish than decoding. Such linguistic features inform the methods and development of reading instruction.

Listening, Reading, Writing, Speaking

Knowing beforehand the structure of the test

Familiarize yourself with the structure of test. It is important to know about the different sections of the tests; if the test is timed as whole or by sections; what is the format for the answers (multiple choice, one-sentence answers, one-paragraph answers, a combination of them). For the writing sections, will the test require a minimum and/or a maximum number of words? Also, inquire whether the test will be done on a computer, on paper, or a combination of both. If computerized, make sure your typing skills are up to the task, both in speed and in accuracy, and learn and practice in advance the particular keys you have to use to write those Spanish letters and characters (á, é, í, ó, ú, ñ, ¿, ¡) that do not exist in English.

Importance of timing during tests

Most tests you will take will be timed. Some of them allocate a certain amount of time for the whole test and let you decide how much time you will spend in each section. Others will be more structured and will assign specific time for each section. In both cases, you have to perform a series of tasks (reading, writing, listening, answering multiple-choice or essay questions, etc.) in the time you have been given. It is very important you know how much time you have and how to best use it. Organize yourself: give yourself time to think, to draft, and to review. Do not rush but do not spend too much time on a certain point either. If you see you are running out of time, do not panic; your performance will be better if you stay calm.

Missing a particular word when writing or speaking

Many times you will be writing or speaking and you realize you do not know or do not remember a particular word. Do not panic or try stubbornly to get the word, just go around it. For nouns (percha/hanger), describe what the object looks like (un triángulo con un gancho/a triangle with a hook), what it is made of (alambre/wire, madera/wood, o plástico/or plastic) what it is used for (para colgar la ropa/to hang clothes), or where you can find it (en el armario/in the closet). For adjectives, use opposites. For verbs, use the results of the action. Be sure to convey your message with the proper spelling or pronunciation and in a grammatically correct way.

Steps to follow when answering the written exam

The first step for all writing assignments is to carefully read the instructions, making sure you know what is required in terms of content (the topic), style (formal/informal, narrative/description/etc., letter/essay/etc.), and length (minimum and maximum number of words). It is also important to know how much time you have to complete the section of the test. Once you know what you are required to do, start developing and organizing your ideas. Identify which is the main idea and which are secondary or supporting ideas. Make an outline and do not forget the introduction and the conclusion. Following your outline, write a draft of your answer. Finally, revise your draft. Make sure you have done what was required and it has been presented clearly. To finish, edit for clarity and flow, and proofread for grammar, spelling, and punctuation.

Components of your answers in the written exam

The written part of the test will include a variety of styles and requirements: letters, memos, or e-mails; narrative, descriptive, or opinion texts; formal or informal forms of address. In all cases, your ideas have to be organized and neatly stated. Start by presenting your topic and how you plan to develop it. Continue with the main section of your piece where you tell, describe, or explain your point in a logical manner. Wrap it up by presenting your conclusions and results. The length of these three sections, introduction, body, and conclusion, will depend on the number of words required in your assignment. One or two sentences or a short paragraph are the norm for the introduction and the conclusion.

Elements to consider for the written exam

When completing the written exam, there are certain basic elements that should be taken into consideration. They apply to all writing assignments in all languages. Among them:

- Match answer to assignment (content, style, and length)
- Define your purpose
- Consider your audience
- Select your role and tone
- Develop an outline
- Organize the body of the piece (by space, time, emphasis, or other clustering concept)
- Start with an introduction
- End with a conclusion
- Check for unity and coherence
- Proofread for grammar, spelling, and punctuation

Organizational structures used in the body of a written piece

A well-organized body presents your ideas clearly and efficiently. The organization of the body of your text will depend on the topic, your audience, and your purpose. There are several organizational structures that will cover most situations, among them:

- Spatial, used mainly for descriptions of places, objects, and people
- Chronological, used mostly to narrate events or explain a process
- General to specific, used commonly in discussions
- Climactic (in order of increasing importance), usually arranged from most familiar to least familiar or from simplest to most complex

Outline

The outline is one of the most useful tools to build a clear, well-organized piece. It basically lists your ideas in the order they will be covered. It will guide you through your writing and show the relative importance of each element. An outline can be particularly useful to shape the body of your piece. Create a section of the outline for each main idea. Check the order of the sections. Do they follow the order you want (chronological, spatial, from generic to specific, etc.)? Are all of them relevant? Are there any gaps or overlaps? Within each section, add the secondary ideas and the supporting information and examples. Apply the same questions to the secondary ideas and to supporting material. Reorganize as needed. Once your outline is ready, follow its structure to draft your essay.

Introduction

All writing assignments should begin with an introduction. The topic will be described in the test's instructions, but it has to be presented at the beginning of your text. You cannot assume the reader knows the topic, and you cannot start your piece as a continuation of the instructions. You should also include a brief outline of the main points. The introduction should be simple, clear, and concise. Do not use *el propósito de este ensayo es* (the purpose of this essay is), *estoy escribiendo acerca de* (I am writing about), or similar expressions. The length of the introduction will depend on the total number of words required for the particular assignment. Most of the times, one or two sentences are enough. In other cases, a longer paragraph is more appropriate.

Conclusion

All writing assignments should end with a conclusion. The conclusion will wrap up your piece. It will tell the reader you have finished. It should briefly summarize the main points and might include results or a suggested course of action. Do not restate your introduction and do not include new ideas. Try to avoid expressions such as *aunque no soy experto* (although I am not an expert), *yo creo* (I believe), and *en mi opinión* (in my opinion). The length of the conclusion will depend on the total number of words required for the particular assignment. Most of the time, one or two sentences are enough. In other cases, a longer paragraph is more appropriate.

Identifying patterns in written and oral exams

Asking some questions about the information presented in a written or oral piece and paying attention to specific elements will help you identify what type of text you have in front of you. These questions and elements will also help you when you have to write a specific type of text. Some of the more common options are listed below.

- What happened? → narration
- What does it look, sound, smell, or taste like?→ description
- It includes examples or reasons. → illustration/support
- It is like, or different from, something else. → comparison and contrast
- It happened because… → cause and effect
- What is it? → definition
- It states opinions. → position
- How to do it. → process analysis

Writing process

The writing process consists of three basic stages: development, drafting, and revision. Following these three steps will help you write a well-rounded piece. During the development, you will find and gather information about your topic. You will then select the most relevant information and organize it in an outline. In the drafting stage, you will write your ideas based on the information collected during development, explaining and connecting them. During the revision, you will go through your text, rethinking and rewriting to improve the overall structure and content, editing for clarity and flow, and proofreading for grammar, spelling, and punctuation.

Writing situation

The writing situation refers to your subject and your audience and will help you present the subject to the audience in the most appropriate way. The subject will be provided in the instructions. Make sure you write about what you are required. If the subject is too broad or general, focus on a specific part of the subject, narrowing it to a topic that can be properly addressed in the essay you are writing. In most cases, your audience will be also defined in your assignment. If not, consider the general public with no in-depth knowledge of the particular subject as your audience.

Knowing your audience

Knowing who you are writing for is a very important element for any type of writing assignment. In general, your audience will be defined or implied in the instructions. All good written pieces match the information and the way it is presented to the designated audience. Too much, too detailed, or too specific information may not be appropriate for a general audience. Too general or too little information will not suit a knowledgeable audience. The format and style you use to present the information should also match the audience. Informal, personal sentences are fitting for an e-mail to a friend or family member. A formal tone is required for a letter to a future employer. If you cannot identify your audience from the instructions, consider it as the general public with no in-depth knowledge of your particular subject.

Importance of unity and coherence

Unity and coherence are the two elements that will make a written or oral piece flow smoothly. When checking for unity, see if all parts of the piece support the main idea. All examples and details should be relevant to the central idea. All sections of your piece should relate to each other. If a piece is coherent, the reader/listener will be able to see relations and easily go from one thought to another one. Organize your material in a logical manner. Check for gaps and abrupt transitions and add connective words or phrases to guide the reader along your thinking path.

Revision and editing

It is very important that you have time to revise and edit your written assignments. In this last step, you will be able to correct any mistakes, omissions, or other errors that you overlooked while writing. When revising and editing check that:

- The subject of your piece matches your assignment
- You have answered all questions and included everything that was requested
- You have followed the instructions regarding format
- You have used the appropriate style and tone for your audience
- You have used the right vocabulary and clear and readable language
- Your piece is well-organized
- There are appropriate transitions between paragraphs
- Your grammar is correct
- There are no misspelled words
- You have used the correct punctuation

Summarizing a written or oral piece

You may be asked to summarize a written or oral piece. In doing so, you are being asked to state the same ideas as developed in the piece but in a much more concise form. The amount of information you include in a summary depends on the length allowed for it. Go through the text and find the main ideas. State them as briefly as possible. If you were allotted a small amount of words, the main ideas will be all you can include in the summary. If you still have room, go through the text again and find secondary ideas. Pick up the important ones and include them in the summary, also as briefly and clearly as possible. Make sure you are true to the text. Do not include details and do not add new ideas or your own opinions.

Developing an opinion or position piece

You may be asked to develop a piece based on your own personal opinions about a certain subject. In the introduction, you should start by briefly stating your point of view. The body of the piece should describe your opinion in detail, explaining and justifying it, and refuting any objections. The body should also include examples and material from other sources to support your opinion. Create an outline to make sure your arguments are organized in a clear, logical manner. Avoid using an aggressive tone and attacking other perspectives. Finish the piece restating your opinion and adding possible future actions, if applicable.

Comparison and contrast pieces

Comparison and contrast pieces describe similarities and differences among ideas, people, or things. The introduction should state the subjects and a general description of what features you will compare. For the body, the two most commonly used ways to develop comparisons and contrasts are subject-by-subject and point-by-point. In subject-by-subject, each subject is discussed separately, with a full description of one and then the other. When using this method, keep the order of the elements you compare in the same order for both subjects. In the point-by-point method, the two subjects are discussed at the same time, each element covered for both subject side by side. Examples are usually very useful to clarify ideas in this kind of piece. Finish the piece with your conclusion.

Describing a process

When you explain how to perform a task or how something works, you are describing a process. The first step would be to analyze and fully understand the process. Once familiar with the process you can describe it in a chronological or in spatial way. The method you choose will depend on your subject. Chronologically, you will explain the different steps as they occurred in time, first to last. Spatially, you will organize the information relatively to its physical position (from left to right, for example). For each step, besides defining it and regardless of the method you use, state its purpose and provide any necessary context to make it clear.

Writing memos

A memo (short for memorandum) is usually a short, concise written piece used at work to inform, instruct, or remind about a particular subject. Memos do not have to be very formal, but they do not tend to be very informal either. They must be very clear. The heading of a memo should start with the date, the recipient, and the sender. Include a subject line at the beginning, describing in a few words the topic of the memo (see example of heading below). Use short paragraphs and simple sentences. Include lists and use specific vocabulary. Avoid the passive voice and unnecessary details. Memos do not include a salutation nor signature at the bottom.

MEMORANDUM

July 13, 2012

To: Paul Johnson

From: Lisa Smith

SUBJECT: Personnel changes

Writing e-mails

Nowadays, e-mail is the most common written mode of communication for both personal and business purposes. As with letters, the format and style of an e-mail will depend on the relationship between the sender and the recipient. Family members and friends will use a very informal, colloquial language. E-mails sent to a company asking for a job will be as formal and structured as a letter of inquiry. Read your assignment carefully, and determine how the sender and recipient are related. Use the degree of formality that matches that relationship. Whether formal or informal, organize your thoughts and present them in a clear, logical manner.

Narrations

A narration answers the question, "What happened?" The subject is developed as a story or a sequence of events. The events can be real or fictional. A narration is commonly organized in chronological order, especially in the short pieces you will be asked to write. Narrations are usually written in the first or third person. Since you will be writing about situations that might occur at different times, make sure you use the correct tense for all verbs and that they correlate to the different points in time associated with each action.

Writing descriptions

A description answers the question, "What does it look like?" It can also responds to "What does it smell, sound, taste, or feel like?" A description can be subjective or objective, depending on whether you use your opinions in the essay. A description can be organized relative to space, as from right to left or from top to bottom; from the whole to the parts, as when you describe the general shape of a face and then the eyes, mouth, nose, etc.; or for emphasis, where you start with the most important or relevant traits and then go into other features.

Cause and effect pieces

Cause-and-effect or cause-and-consequence pieces answer basically to the question "Why?" You will analyze and present why something happened or what is likely to happen. It is very important that you keep your ideas very well organized. Do not mix causes and effects. To avoid confusions and misinterpretations, keep as much as possible in the same sentence or paragraph each cause and its effect or consequence and the supporting information. It will be better in most cases also to focus either on the causes or on the effects. Some useful expressions for this type of piece are: *porque, dado que, entonces, así que, debido a, por lo tanto, por eso, por causa de*, etc.

Reading Comprehension questions

During the test, you will be given a passage to read. You will have to answer a series of multiple-choice questions or write an answer based on that text. Read carefully through the passage to grasp and understand its content. Find primary and secondary ideas as well as supporting information and examples. Pay attention to style and tone. Is it written in a formal or a familiar style? Is it polite, authoritarian, or ironic? Is it written in simple or scholarly language? All these elements are cues that you can use to infer information not specifically written in the text but still included in the passage and that will help you better understand the text.

Listening Comprehension questions

During the test, you will listen to a text or conversation. You will have to answer a series of multiple-choice questions or write an answer based on what you heard. Listen carefully throughout the passage to grasp and understand its content. It may help to take notes as you listen. Find the primary and secondary ideas as well as supporting information and examples. Pay attention to style and tone. Is it a formal passage? Does it sound friendly? Does it use simple language? All these elements are cues that you can use to infer information not explicitly stated in the text but still included in the passage. The better you understand the text, the more accurate your answers will be.

Multiple-choice question after reading/listening to a passage

Carefully read/listen to the passage a first time. Read the questions and answer those you are sure about. Make notes about the possible answers to those questions you have doubts about or do not know. Do not spend too much time on any particular question. Read/listen to the passage again, concentrating on finding the missing answers. Go through the questions again and answer them. In most cases, two readings will be enough to complete all questions. If not, reread/listen to the passage and go over the missing answers one more time. Read/listen to the passage one final time. Revise and do a final check on your answers.

Speaking Tasks

The test will include several Speaking Tasks, and you will have some time to prepare for them. During the preparation, make sure that:

- you accurately respond to the content, audience, style, and format requirements
- you present your ideas in an organized, logical manner
- your speech is coherent and has unity (flows smoothly)
- you use the correct words (vocabulary) and grammar

When you deliver your speaking task, make sure that:

- you speak clearly
- you speak neither too fast nor to slow
- you pay close attention to pronunciation

Simulated Conversation section

You might be asked to simulate a conversation in Spanish. You will be given an outline of the conversation. The outline will not give you the exact words that you will hear but just a general idea of what you can expect. You will have a certain time to prepare and deliver your part of the conversation after each line. Listen carefully to the first line of the conversation. Look for the main topic and who the other person is. Pay attention to use of *tú* vs. *usted* and to familiar words and expressions. Note regional cues, educational level of the language, and tone used by the other person. All these elements will help you choose the appropriate content, style, and tone you will use in your answers.

Process to follow for an oral presentation

You may be asked to orally express an opinion on a given topic. You will have some time to prepare your response. Read/listen carefully to the statement defining the topic. List the main points. Explain your opinion, justify it, and refute objections. Support your opinion with examples or by mentioning other available sources. Organize your arguments in a clear, logical manner. Avoid attacking other perspectives. You can finish your presentation by adding possible future actions.

When delivering your speech, avoid using an aggressive tone or getting emotional. Speak clearly and not too fast but not too slow either. Pay special attention to your pronunciation.

Listening comprehension, context, tone, and intonation

For the listening comprehension section, it is very important to pay attention to the general context of the narration, description, conversation, or statement. Understanding context is extremely helpful to infer the meaning of words you might not know. It also helps to determine the appropriate meaning for those words that have more than one (*cara*: expensive or face; *frente*: front or forehead). The tone used in an oral piece (happy, serious, ironic, formal) will be another tool to assess the situation. Intonation will help you determine the tense (*hablo* → present and *habló* → past) and if a sentence is an affirmative or a question. Emphasis on particular words will give you clues of what is important (*mi lápiz es azul*/my pencil not my pen; *mi lápiz es azul*/it is blue not red).

Reading comprehension, informative and persuasive styles

When reading a text, it is important to determine the style of the piece. In the informative style, the author presents the information and the data in an objective way. He/she is trying to educate or give something to the audience. On the other hand, in the persuasive style, the writer is trying to convince the reader of his/hers ideas. He/she presents the information from his/her own point of view. In a piece written in the persuasive style, it is important to be able to separate the actual facts from the opinions of the author.

Listening and reading comprehension, main ideas

The first step when reading or listening to a text is to identify the main idea(s) of the piece. In many cases, not everything will be clearly stated. Secondary ideas and supporting examples will help you to infer content within the context of the text. Finding out who the audience is, to whom the piece is intended, and the style and tone of the text will give a more accurate indication of the purpose of the material. It is also important to pay attention to the sequence of events and to cause-and-effect relationships to be able to answer questions properly.

MTTC Practice Test

Section 1 – Listening and Cultural Knowledge

In the listening section of the test you will hear several texts, dialogues and conversations recorded by native Spanish speakers; you will then have to answer multiple choice questions based on the material you have heard. With so many Spanish speaking countries, each one with its own particular accent, expressions, and vocabulary, you will have to listen carefully as the pronunciations will differ, and there may be different words and phrases to describe the same object, action or quality. You will listen to each selection twice, with a brief break between them to look at the questions. After the second time, the questions will be shown on the screen one by one. You will have to answer them as they come up, and you will not be able to go back.

The selections are real spoken language; therefore they will vary in structure, delivery and content. They can be chats, interviews, dialogues and other oral interactive exchanges of two or more people. They can also be presentations, lectures, or readings by only one speaker. They can be formal or informal; it can be a cultured delivery or just a plain, everyday conversation. The speakers may talk slowly and clearly, fast and linking words, or hesitantly and with pauses and repetitions. There may be background noise too (cars, other people talking or music). As for content, the topics are endless.

The questions will be aimed at evaluating your understanding of the spoken language and cultural knowledge. Most questions will be quite similar to those used in Section 2 – Reading with Cultural Knowledge, and will include not only those that test your comprehension of the selection but also linguistic aspects (meaning of words and expressions, differences among countries), text structure and format (ideas presented in order of importance, in chronological order, etc.), and type (narration, description, debate). Additionally, however, there will be questions that apply only to spoken language such as:

- Does the speaker sound friendly, aggressive?
- Is the speaker a child, a teenager, a grown up, an old person?
- Is the speaker in a hurry, bored?
- Does the speaker sound comfortable, tired?

Remember that spoken language is not perfect: you are trying to express yourself on the fly and you cannot go back to fix the errors. When talking, even the most educated person makes minor mistakes, uses incomplete sentences and leaves ideas dangling.

To practice for this part of the test, ask different native Spanish speakers you may know to engage in conversations of various types, to make a presentation or to read a text of their choice. Listen carefully and try to pick up the differences in accents, expressions, and word selection. You can also listen to the radio or watch TV shows and news in Spanish. Switch channels to expose yourself to different countries. Watch a Mexican soap opera, a Colombian beauty pageant, Argentinean news, the Puerto Rican weather forecast. Again, pay attention to how they speak, the terms they use, their idioms, and, after listening for a while, try to answer the type of questions mentioned above.

Section 2 – Reading with Cultural Knowledge

Text #1

Enclavado en el mismo centro viejo de Madrid, lleno de voces, colores y aromas, El Rastro es un típico mercado al aire libre ubicado en el pintoresco y sonoro antiguo barrio judío de Lavapiés. Comenzó como un zoco tradicional de venta de artículos de segunda mano alrededor de 1740, y creció y se diversificó a través de los años hasta alcanzar hoy en día 3500 puestos.

La variedad de objetos ofrecidos es impresionante. Se pueden encontrar todo tipo de antigüedades (muebles de estilo, candiles antiguos, cuadros de tiempos pasados) en diversas condiciones de mantenimiento. Algunos de los objetos están tan bien conservados que parecen recién hechos. Otros se ven tan viejos y polvorientos que uno se pregunta quién puede tener interés en comprar un trasto en tan mal estado. Otro rubro muy bien representado es el de ropa y accesorios personales. Abundan pendientes, botones, colgantes, carteras, zapatos, gorras y sombreros, chales y chaquetas de toda época. Pero no todo es antiguo. Hay también puestos de artículos electrónicos de segunda mano, desguace de automóviles, y artesanías locales modernas. Si te decides a comprar algo, siguiendo la mejor tradición moruna de este tipo de mercado, el regateo es de rigor. El precio inicial es sólo el punto de partida para una serie de tira y afloja hasta llegar al acuerdo final.

Funciona los domingos y feriados desde la mañana y hasta después del almuerzo, y su fama es tal que no hay guía turística de Madrid que no lo incluya. Los locales acostumbran visitarlo también regularmente. Prefieren hacerlo los domingos temprano cuando hay más para ver y disfrutar, ya que alrededor de las dos de la tarde muchos de los puestos comienzan ya a recoger sus mercancías, y la gente y el bullicio dan lugar a un paisaje un poco desolado. Las reglamentaciones municipales no permiten puestos de alimentos y de animales vivos pero es muy fácil hacer un alto en el paseo y encontrar en el área dónde gustar los típicos barquillos madrileños o reparar a una auténtica tasca para tomar un aperitivo con tapas con los amigos luego de una mañana de exploración y vuelta al pasado.

Responder a las preguntas siguientes basándose en el texto anterior.

1. Un "zoco" es:
   a. Mercado de pulgas judío
   b. Mercado de pequeñas comunidades madrileñas
   c. Bazar tradicional de los países árabes
   d. Mercado de artesanos nativos

2. El texto indica que El Rastro fue creado:
   a. En el siglo XVII
   b. Por los moros
   c. En el siglo XVIII
   d. Por los judíos españoles

- 88 -

3. De acuerdo al texto, en El Rastro se pueden comprar, entre otras cosas:
   a. Antigüedades y objetos de época
   b. Comidas y bebidas
   c. Productos artesanales importados
   d. Todo lo anterior

4. El Rastro está abierto:
   a. Todas la mañanas
   b. Todos los domingos y días festivos
   c. Todos los domingos y días festivos a la mañana
   d. Los días feriados desde la mañana y hasta media tarde

5. El texto señala el uso del regateo en El Rastro. ¿Qué entiende usted por esto?
   a. La reducción del precio de un artículo
   b. La confirmación del precio de un artículo
   c. La negociación del precio de un artículo
   d. El cambio de unidad monetaria del precio de un artículo

6. Los "locales" mencionados en la segunda oración del último párrafo se refieren a:
   a. Los artesanos de la zona que venden sus productos en El Rastro
   b. Los madrileños que visitan El Rastro
   c. Las costumbres de los madrileños
   d. Los barquillos y otras comidas típicas

Text #2

Violeta Parra nació en 1917 en un pequeño pueblo en un área rural a unos 300 km al sur de Santiago en una prolífica familia de poetas, folcloristas y artistas. Pasó su infancia en el campo y, adolescente, se mudó a Santiago para vivir con su hermano y retomar sus estudios después de la muerte de su padre. No estando interesada en estudiar sino en el canto, abandonó la escuela y empezó a cantar con su hermana en pequeños bares, lugares de recreo y salones de barrio. Se casó con un empleado ferroviario y tuvo dos hijos, pero su primer matrimonio no duró demasiado debido a la vida inquieta y poco convencional de Violeta. Al principio de los años 50, impulsada por su amor al canto y al folclore, comenzó a recopilar tradiciones musicales a lo largo del país, las que resultaron en su libro *Cantos Folclóricos Chilenos* y en sus primeros discos. Viajó a Europa y a la Unión Soviética, y aprovechó estos viajes para grabar en Paris. De vuelta en Chile, fundó el Museo Nacional de Arte Folclórico en la ciudad de Concepción. Siguió cantando y grabando, y vivió durante un tiempo en Argentina con dos de sus hijos. Continuó viajando por Europa y expuso obras en el Louvre.

Aun cuando su obra incluye numerosos trabajos de calidad como artista plástica (pinturas, esculturas, cerámicas, bordados), Violeta Parra es mundialmente conocida por sus canciones. Su canción más famosa, *Gracias a la Vida*, fue popularizada en Latinoamérica por Mercedes Sosas y Alberto Cortez, y en Los Estados Unidos por Joan Baez. En la canción, himno folclórico celebrando la vida, Parra utiliza un lirismo romántico para agradecer a ésta la vista y el oído que le permiten apreciar lo que hay a su alrededor, y la voz, el corazón, la risa y el llanto que le permiten expresar sus sentimientos. Lamentablemente, un año después de

- 89 -

componer *Gracias a la Vida*, y según algunos debido a desengaños amorosos, Parra se quitó la vida de un tiro en la cabeza. No alcanzó a cumplir los 50 años. Se ha dicho que en realidad, la intención de Parra al escribir la canción fue como nota de despedida, señalando, irónicamente, que buena salud, oportunidades y éxitos personales a nivel mundial no son suficientes para sobrellevar el dolor de la condición humana.

Responder a las preguntas siguientes basándose en el texto anterior.

1. Violeta Parra nació en
   a. Argentina
   b. Chile
   c. Perú
   d. Uruguay

2. Se puede inferir del texto que Violeta Parra:
   a. Nunca estuvo casada
   b. Estuvo casada una vez
   c. Estuvo casada dos veces
   d. Estuvo casada más de una vez

3. De acuerdo al texto, en su canción más famosa, Violeta Parra agradece:
   a. Estar viva
   b. Poder expresar sus sentimientos
   c. Los cinco sentidos
   d. El ser amado

4. Violeta Parra murió:
   a. De pena, después de un desengaño amoroso
   b. A consecuencia de un accidente con un arma de fuego
   c. Se suicidó
   d. Como resultado de una tumor en la cabeza

5. Lirismo se refiere a:
   a. Unión inefable del alma con Dios
   b. Ideal fundamental de equilibrio y sobriedad y de fidelidad a la naturaleza
   c. Imitación de modelos de la antigüedad
   d. Subjetividad en la expresión musical

6. Las ideas del primer párrafo están organizadas:
   a. En orden de importancia creciente
   b. En orden de importancia decreciente
   c. En orden temporal
   d. No tienen ningún orden particular

Text #3

El petróleo es un material orgánico generado por la descomposición de microorganismos provenientes de la tierra, el mar o lagos y que han sido enterrados bajo pesadas capas de sedimentos y cocinados a altas temperaturas durante miles

- 90 -

de años. Está compuesto por largas cadenas de hidrógeno y carbono y pequeñas cantidades de nitrógeno, oxígeno y azufre. Una vez generado en la roca madre, rica en microorganismos, el petróleo migra hacia una zona permeable donde, atrapado por capas selladoras impermeables, es almacenado en los poros del reservorio. Si los organismos son sometidos a mayores temperaturas, las cadenas se rompen y, dados la temperatura y el tiempo necesarios, se transforma en gas, el cual está formado por los mismos elementos básicos que el petróleo pero en arreglos de cadenas mucho más cortas. Aunque originalmente formado a grandes profundidades bajo la corteza terrestre, los movimientos de ésta, tales como terremotos, levantamientos y desplazamientos, hacen que se pueda encontrar más cerca de la superficie.

Utilizando pruebas sísmicas, los geólogos estudian la distribución y tipos de rocas debajo de la superficie para localizar probables zonas donde el petróleo puede haberse depositado. Para extraerlo, se perfora un pozo en la tierra hasta llegar al reservorio. El pozo es bastante ancho en la superficie (de hasta 36 pulgadas) pero su diámetro disminuye a medida que se alcanzan profundidades mayores, llegando a ser a veces de sólo 7 pulgadas. Durante la perforación se circula dentro del pozo una mezcla de fluidos, sólidos y productos químicos llamado lodo de perforación. Este lodo está especialmente formulado para cada pozo para enfriar la broca, traer los cortes de roca a la superficie y mantener la presión adecuada. El pozo es entubado con cañerías para, entre otras cosas, prevenir desmoronamientos de las paredes del pozo dentro del mismo, evitar que agua, petróleo y gas almacenados en las formaciones rocosas entre en el pozo, y aislar las distintas capas de rocas unas de otras.

Durante y una vez terminada la perforación, se bajan herramientas de ensayo dentro del pozo para correr pruebas y establecer si hay petróleo y a qué profundidad. En caso de encontrarse una capa productiva, se baja una herramienta especial que contienen explosivos para perforar la cañería a la profundidad deseada y deja entrar el petróleo al pozo.

Responder a las preguntas siguientes basándose en el texto anterior

1. El petróleo está formado por:
   a. organismos terrestres
   b. organismos marinos
   c. organismos lacustres
   d. todos los anteriores

2. El petróleo se acumula en:
   a. la roca madre
   b. las capas selladoras
   c. la superficie de la tierra
   d. el reservorio

3. Para obtener gas hace falta:

a. mayor temperatura y más tiempo que para obtener petróleo
b. mayor temperatura y menos tiempo que para obtener petróleo
c. menor temperatura y más tiempo que para obtener petróleo
d. menor temperatura y menos tiempo que para obtener petróleo

4. Los estudios sísmicos

a. indican con exactitud dónde hay petróleo
b. producen terremotos
c. ayudan a determinar las características de las rocas subterráneas
d. son realizados dentro del pozo

5. La función del lodo de perforación es:

a. enfriar la broca — drill bit
b. evitar el desmoronamiento del pozo
c. aislar las diferentes capas rocosas unas de otras
d. profundizar el pozo

6. El texto es:

a. una narración
b. un descripción
c. una debate
d. un análisis de causa y efecto

Text #4

La lufa es el fruto de una planta enredadera tropical que se puede encontrar en forma salvaje en la selva amazónica. Es originaria de la India y fue introducida en Ecuador desde Colombia. Se parece a una calabaza, con un interior en forma de tubo hecho de fibras cortas naturalmente tejidas, y sus propiedades para el cuidado y exfoliación de la piel y para la activación de la circulación han sido reconocidas. Hoy en día es cultivada por unas 500 familias de agricultores en el valle de Manduriacos y comercializada por la cooperativa local Taller de la Lufa.

Una vez que se han recogido los frutos, éstos se ponen en remojo para poder quitar más fácilmente la cáscara gruesa que los recubre. Se eliminan también las semillas y se ponen a secar los frutos al sol. Una vez finalizado este lavado y secado, están listos para ser llevados a lomo de mula hasta el Taller. El Taller de la Lufa arregla un precio justo con los campesinos locales para la compra de la cosecha y provee el material para que los artesanos la combinen con algodón crudo, hilo de abacá, fibra de plátano y madera de balsa, entre otros materiales, para fabricar todo tipo de artículos para el baño, entre ellos esponjas, zapatillas y cepillos. También, después de un segundo lavado y de un planchado con rodillos metálicos, y usando tinturas de colores vivos se la usa para hacer cortinas, alfombras y adornos.

La mayor parte de los productos son exportados. Los principales compradores son los Estados Unidos y el Japón, pero ciertas líneas han tenido un gran éxito en España y Francia. De a poco, la penetración en el mercado nacional va incrementando. El Taller no sólo compra la cosecha de los agricultores y vende los productos fabricados por los artesanos, sino también asesora a ambos sobre calidad, precio y comercialización de sus productos.

Parte de las ganancias del Taller se reinvierten en el mismo, para mejorar sus instalaciones y equipos. Otra parte se utiliza para obras de ayuda social de los pueblos u obras de interés general. Con estos fondos se ha comprado un camión para ayudar a la gente a vender su producción en lugares más alejados donde pueden conseguir mejor precio por su producto. También se han reparado puentes y otras estructuras locales. En este momento el Taller tiene planeado construir una planta de secado de cacahuetes, desarrollar una empresa de turismo responsable, y construir un centro residencial-educativo.

Responder a las preguntas siguientes basándose en el texto anterior

1. La lufa se encuentra en forma salvaje en la selva amazónica significa que ésta crece:

    a. De forma desenfrenada
    b. De forma ilimitada
    c. De forma silvestre
    d. De forma irresponsable

2. Las esponjas de lufa son buenas para:

    a. Perder peso
    b. Eliminar las arrugas
    c. Remojarse la piel
    d. Quitar células muertas

3. El proceso de preparación de la lufa para la fabricación de artículos de baño es:

    a. Lavado
    b. Lavado y secado
    c. Lavado, secado y planchado
    d. Lavado, planchado y secado

4. El Taller de la Lufa es:

    a. Una compañía privada
    b. Una empresa pública
    c. Una entidad del estado
    d. Una cooperativa local

5. Los agricultores llevan sus productos a otros lugares alejados porque:

    a. El Taller de la Lufa no les compra la cosecha
    b. El Taller de la Lufa paga muy poco
    c. Otros compradores pagan más
    d. No se llevan bien con el Taller d la Lufa

6. El centro residencial-educativo planeado por el Taller de la Lufa es:

    a. Un complejo donde los estudiantes residen y estudian
    b. Una escuela ubicada en un barrio residencial
    c. Un centro para la educación de los habitantes de un barrio residencial
    d. Sólo para los estudiantes que no residen en la escuela

Text #5

Con el título de "El Renacimiento del Fresco en México", publicó en Le Cahier, famoso mensual de Parias, el año pasado, un interesante artículo el inteligente crítico y musicógrafo cubano Alejo Carpentier.

Da ocasión ese artículo para efectuar serias meditaciones sobre la vigorosa personalidad de Diego de Rivera, quien ha conquistado primero un renombre universal y comienza a tener popularidad en su adorado México.

Discutir la personalidad de Diego de Rivera, es ahora materia de varios volúmenes, así de proteica, complicada, variable y grandiosa. Alejo Carpentier, ha logrado, no obstante, efectuar una síntesis de todas las calidades de Diego en unas cuantas líneas; ellas revelan, al punto, la magnitud de este artista nuevo.

Diego es el poeta de la fuerza, de la grandiosidad social, del hecho conscientemente mexicanos; sus frescos, están hechos por un hombre, lleno de potencia creadora. Se ve en ellos la intención humana, cosmológica, social; se siente al contemplarlos el misterio de una aurora que brilla como algo nuevo en el alma.

El renacimiento del fresco en México es una realidad que tiene como principalísimo responsable a Diego aunque en esta hora hay otros pintores de murales con calidades tan valiosas como las que se encuentran en Diego; pero está fuera de discusión que sin el arrojo, la perseverancia, el gesto bélico y otras circunstanciás extraestéticas de Rivera, ese renacimiento no hubiera sido posible en esta época.

Pendiente de terminación la obra de colosales dimensiones que ha emprendido Diego en el Palacio Nacional, se ha dedicado en los últimos meses a pintar las paredes del Palacio de Gobierno del Estado de Morelos en la pintoresca Ciudad de Cuernavaca.

Esta obra, es un obsequio del Embajador de los E.U.A., en la república Mexicana a la Nación, pues por se cuenta la ejecuta Diego. Mr. Morrow ha sido uno de sus más adictos admiradores.

[....]

Se sigue notando en Diego el gusto por las actitudes combativas, caricaturescas, ridiculizantes, terriblemente irónicas. Esa cabeza de Hernán Cortés, visible en estas reproducciones, dice más sobre la ideología universal de Diego que todos sus discursos y declaraciones.

Desgraciadamente, esta preocupación ideológica hace desmerecer la obra de Diego en su calidad estética, hace a uno pensar, aun sin quererlo, en monstruosas ilustraciones de libros o en escenografía teatral.

Responder a las preguntas siguientes basándose en el texto anterior

1. Alejo Carpentier publicó un artículo sobre el renacimiento de los frescos en Méjico en:
   a. Méjico
   b. Cuba
   c. Francia
   d. Los Estados Unidos

2. De acuerdo al texto, la personalidad de Diego de Rivera es:
   a. Débil
   b. Simple
   c. Estable
   d. Ninguna de las anteriores

3. Diego de Rivera es responsable del renacimiento en Méjico:
   a. De las artes plásticas
   b. Del muralismo
   c. De las actitudes ridiculizantes
   d. De la pintura social

4. En el momento en que se escribió este texto, Diego de Rivera estaba trabajando en un fresco
   a. En la ciudad de Cuernavaca
   b. En el palacio de Gobierno de Morelos
   c. Pagado por un extranjero
   d. Todas las anteriores

5. A Diego de Rivera le gustan las imágenes:
   a. Serias
   b. Burlonas
   c. Plácidas
   d. De cabezas grandes

6. El artículo considera los frescos de Diego de Rivera:
   a. Importantes para Méjico
   b. Grandes pero poco significativos
   c. De poca monta
   d. Coloridos y simpáticos

Text #6

Hoy en día, más y más mujeres están cargo de su vida financiera. Algunas lo han hecho desde siempre. Otras se han visto obligadas a hacerlo debido a situaciones de la vida tales como no casarse, divorcio, muerte o incapacidad del esposo. Otras van de a poco tomando más responsabilidades, compartiendo decisiones. Aun cuando a veces lo ven como una tarea extra que se agrega a la larga lista de cosas por hacer, en el fondo están orgullosas de ponerse a la par de los hombres en una actividad de la que se han visto relegadas en muchísimas ocasiones.

Si bien algunas no están interesadas, la falta de participación no es buena. La mujer debe estar informada acerca de sus asuntos financieros. ¿Cuánto dinero entra en la casa mensualmente? ¿Cuánto hace falta para pagar las cuentas todos los meses? ¿Tiene deudas? ¿Cuánto puede ahorrar? ¿Tiene dinero invertido? Éstas son algunas preguntas básicas que toda mujer debe saber responder.

Un mayor conocimiento de la situación la hará sentirse más confiada y proclive a profundizar más en el asunto. El próximo paso sería definir sus objetivos financieros. ¿Qué quiere hacer? ¿Eliminar las deudas? ¿Ahorrar para pagar la educación de los hijos? ¿Tener lo suficiente como para vivir cómodamente una vez que se retire? La mujer tiene que estar informada y es mejor que tome parte en estas decisiones.

Una vez que ha decidido lo que se quiere, hay que decidir cómo lograrlo. Normalmente, ésta es la parte que más intimida ya que la cantidad y variedad de opciones es apabullante. Tarjetas de crédito y de débito, cuentas corrientes, cuentas de ahorro, depósitos a plazo fijo, cuentas de inversión, acciones, fondos, bonos, anualidades. Cada banco e institución financiera ofrece su propio menú. ¿Cómo manejarse con tantas cosas diferentes? Es aquí donde la ayuda de un profesional financiero hace la diferencia. Un consultor financiero ha estudiado profundamente todos estos aspectos y tiene a su alcance las herramientas apropiadas para realizar una evaluación realística de la situación y de los objetivos. Una vez realizado el análisis, el consultor puede ofrecerle los vehículos adecuados para alcanzar lo que desea.

Gómez, Gónzalez y Rodriguez es una firma especializada en análisis financieros. Sus consultores han sido capacitados para estudiar detalladamente su situación y objetivos financieros a corto y largo plazo. Todos los consultores tienen amplio conocimiento de lo que el mercado financiero ofrece, y no se detienen hasta encontrar las mejores opciones para usted y su familia. Su futuro y seguridad financieros están a su alcance. No espere más; llámenos por teléfono o pase por nuestras oficinas donde siempre encontrará un consultor a su disposición.

Responder a las preguntas siguientes basándose en el texto anterior

1. Algunas de las mujeres ven las responsabilidades financieras como:
   a. Una carga extra
   b. Un deber
   c. Un derecho
   d. Una opción

2. Las mujeres que están a cargo de sus finanzas lo hacen porque:
   a. No tienen permitido contratar a un consultor que las ayude
   b. Es importante tener conocimiento y control de su propia vida financiera
   c. Una nueva ley las obliga a hacerlo
   d. No tienen nada mejor que hacer

3. De acuerdo al texto, una de las cuestiones básicas que toda mujer debería saber es:
   a. Cómo ahorrar
   b. Para qué ahorrar
   c. Cuánto ahorrar
   d. Por qué ahorrar

4. la cantidad y variedad de opciones financieras son:

  a. Muy limitadas
  b. Sólo conocidas por los consultores
  c. Abrumadoras
  d. Fuera del alcance de las mujeres

5. Los consultores financieros pueden:

  a. Ayudar a invertir el dinero
  b. Analizar los objetivos financieros
  c. Evaluar la situación financiera
  d. Todo lo anterior

6. El texto:

  a. Informa a las mujeres de sus derechos financieros
  b. Dice que las mujeres son financieramente incapaces
  c. Es un aviso de una consultoría financiera
  d. Recluta mujeres para trabajar en firmas financieras

Visual #1

¿Cuál de las opciones siguientes describe de mejor manera esta pintura de Emanuel Leutze de 1843?

    a. Fernando de Magallanes presentando a los reyes de España los primeros nativos traídos de América.

    b. Galileo Galilei retractándose de su teoría de que la Tierra gira alrededor del Sol ante los Reyes Católicos.

    c. Hernán Cortés explicando a la reina Sofía y al rey Juan Carlos de España por qué no pudo traer oro y plata del nuevo continente.

    d. Cristóbal Colón solicitando a Isabel de Castilla y a Fernando de Aragón fondos para financiar su viaje a las Indias.

Visual #2

La foto anterior, tomada en 1912 por la expedición de Bingham, muestra las ruinas de:

a. Machu Pichu, la ciudad perdida de los incas, construida en Perú en el siglo XV.
b. Teotihuacán, un templo construido por los mayas en el siglo XVII en Colombia.
c. Un templo construido por los indios patagones en Bolivia.
d. Un templo construido por los conquistadores españoles para los dioses aztecas en el siglo XII.

Visual #3

La pintura *La Posta de San Luis* de Juan León Pallière reproducida aquí representa:

a. Gauchos comiendo después de una jineteada
b. Viajeros alimentándose en un alto en el camino
c. Jinetes recuperándose después de la doma de caballos
d. Campesinos descansando después del arreo de ganado

Section 3: Writing

Essay

Escriba un texto de por lo menos 120 palabras sobre el siguiente tema.

Durante muchos años, el petróleo y el carbón han sido los combustibles principales utilizados para la generación de energía eléctrica. En la última década, el gas ha ido reclamando su parte del mercado. Aun cuando la tecnología geotérmica y la de mareas no son todavía económicamente viables, otras fuentes de energía renovables tales como viento y sol han ido incrementando poco a poco su importancia como generadoras de electricidad. ¿Le parece que estas fuentes de energía renovables tienen un futuro en los Estados Unidos y en el mundo como generadoras principales de energía eléctrica?

Interpersonal Writing: Response to an email, memo or letter.

Responda a la carta siguiente, declinando la invitación, explicando por qué y sugiriendo una solución.

Bogotá, 12 de enero de 2014

Estimado Dr. López Urrutia:

Del 19 al 23 de agosto de 2014 tendrá lugar en la ciudad de Bogotá el Segundo Congreso Colombiano de Conservación de Recursos Naturales, el foro nacional más importante para todo lo concerniente a la conservación de los recursos naturales, la fauna y la flora.

Visto sus conocimientos y trabajos relacionados con los efectos en los cetáceos de las actividades de exploración y explotación petroleras costa afuera de Colombia, deseamos invitarlo a participar como moderador del panel de discusión abierta "Impactos de las actividades de prospección sísmica en la fauna marina de Colombia". El panel se llevará a cabo el 21 de agosto a las 9 de la mañana y durará aproximadamente una hora. Tentativamente, los panelistas serán el Dr. Carlos Alberto Gutiérrez, la Dra. María de los Ángeles Valdeverde y el Licenciado Augusto Pérez Roldán.

Agradeceríamos confirmación de su participación a la brevedad.

Esperando contar con su presencia, lo saluda muy cordialmente

Alberto Gómez Cabrera

Coordinador General

Asociación Colombiana de Conservación de Recursos Naturales

Interpersonal Writing: Writing task based on a given text

Hoy se le comunicó oficialmente de parte de la Comisión de Amigos del Arte, al pintor David Alfaro Siqueiros, que se le prohibía dar su tercera conferencia sobre arte mejicano. Esta decisión no es más que un resultado de la mojigatería. La citada decisión que cubre de ridículo a la institución arriba mencionada comprueba más que nada que la situación de ciertos problemas no pueden ser encarados sin que los que debieran estar interesados en el asunto decidan eludirlos. Siqueiros ha venido a demostrar a los artistas nuestros la forma en que se realizó el movimiento pictórico más interesante del momento actual. Y ahora se le prohíbe que siga en su ciclo de disertaciones.

[...]

"En esas dos primeras conferencias no yo no hice más que relatar los hechos históricos concretos de los movimientos de pintura monumental en que he participado. Es evidente que esos dos movimientos, considerados como los de mayor trascendencia de la época actual por los más importantes críticos europeos, no se produjeron de manera accidental, sino que responden a realidades sociales fundamentales. Ocultar esas realidades fundamentales, las causas sociales que las impulsaron, los fenómenos políticos que le dieron vida, hubiera sido cometer una innobleza frente a los deseos de la masa intelectual argentina, que anhelaba como tal del mismo, dando, en cambio, solamente una relación cronológica, superficial y, sin sentido alguno. Igual cosa habría acontecido si en el caso del bloque de pintores murales de Los Ángeles me hubiera limitado a hablar de los nombres y de las dimensiones de las obras monumentales realizadas.

Lo que vale fundamentalmente en el movimiento de pintores de Los Ángeles, es precisamente su carácter social. El hecho de que su naturaleza constituye la continuación superada del renacimiento mejicano, en que rectifica los errores del primero, encuentra una técnica correspondiente y toma resueltamente el camino de la ideología revolucionaria y del método dialéctico que corresponde a esa ideología. No decir nada sobre este método dialéctico, por razones de suspicacia política, sería ocultar lo más importante del movimiento plástico contemporáneo que radica precisamente en el uso de un método científico para la producción plástica moderna."

Basándose en el texto anterior, escriba un texto breve de por lo menos 120 palabras defendiendo la siguiente afirmación.

La mayoría de los movimientos artísticos modernos tienen origen en los impulsos revolucionarios de las masas, y su valor radica en haber buscado la expresión plástica que expresa los anhelos de los pueblos y su íntima relación con la vida.

Section 4 – Speaking

The Speaking portion of the test has three parts: two involving presentational skills and one involving interpersonal speaking

In the first presentational task you will be required to discuss a topic related to a passage you have already read in the Writing section. You will have half a minute to read the instructions and one minute to re-read the text. For example:

- Based on the text about El Rastro in Section 2, explain why and what you like and dislike about that kind of market.
- Cooperatives tend to help smaller agricultural communities, especially in less developed areas or in those with a big indigenous population that has fewer resources. Do you think the same model can be applied to other products besides those of the land? Use the text about El Taller de la Lufa in Section 2 as a reference.
- Based on the text on Section 3, do you think that art should not be linked to politics?

In the second presentational task, you will be asked to express your opinion or make a 2-minute presentation about a given topic. You will listen to the topic and, after a pause, to the question. You can practice using a variety of topics such as:

- Some said that James Bond movies are getting harder to follow at times and inconsistent with things that happened in previous ones. *Question*: Do you think this is a problem just with James Bond movies or that it also appears in other series of movies?
- Many Latin-American countries have been developing eco-tourism. They believe it is a good way to increase the influx of hard currency without damaging their environment. *Question*: Do you think eco-tourism really preserves natural resources?
- Smart phones give us the flexibility to communicate with others regardless of where we are. This flexibility also entails being expected to respond from anywhere. Some consider that, whether related to work or of personal character, this expectation of availability at all times is an invasion to our private life. *Question*: Do you feel you have been pushed to respond to others at their convenience and not yours?

The interpersonal speaking part of the test will consist of your participation in a simulated conversation. You will be given an outline of the conversation but not the actual words the other person will use. It may be a conversation between friends, with a colleague, or an interview, for example. Some scenarios you can use to practice with a partner could be:

- You talk with your mother to organize a surprise party for your younger brother.
- You talk with a colleague to set up a meeting to discuss sales goals for the following month.
- A lady stops you in the street and asks you the best way to get to the Museum of Fine Arts.
- You are interviewed for a position as second grade Spanish teacher.

For all three speaking tasks, you will have some time to prepare your answers. Read the instructions carefully. Organize your ideas. You can present them in order of importance, in chronological order or in cause and effect order. Stay true to the topic and question. Say as much as you can, but speak clearly and do not rush.

Section 5 – Curriculum/Instruction

1. Which of the following is the best option to reinforce grammar structures using comparisons as a technique?
   a. Compare expressions from different Spanish-speaking countries
   b. Teach how to make comparisons
   c. Compare two different Spanish grammar points
   d. Point out similarities and differences between Spanish and English to teach grammar structures

2. A Spanish-language instructor would use a total immersion class to:
   a. Improve interpretation skills
   b. Learn different accents
   c. Expand vocabulary
   d. Introduce a new grammar concept

3. Showing authentic Spanish-language videos is best for:
   a. Expanding vocabulary
   b. Assessing listening comprehension skills
   c. Showing cultural differences
   d. Illustrating grammar points

4. An instructor wants to expand the students' vocabulary regarding clothing, which of the following will be the best tool?
   a. Watch a video of a Spanish fashion show
   b. Use the internet to order a piece of clothing from a Mexican website
   c. Give a list of most common clothes
   d. Ask students to describe what they are wearing

5. Written multiple choice questions are the best tool to evaluate:
 a. Writing skills
 b. Interpersonal skills
 c. Grammar skills
 d. Intercommunication skills

6. Which is the most effective technique to introduce the differences between the formal and informal second person of the singular (tú, vos, usted)?
 a. Give a detailed hand-out explaining the different usages
 b. Listen to live recordings of formal and informal situations from different countries
 c. Role-play formal and informal situations
 d. Conduct a discussion about the differences between formal and informal

7. Which of the following is the best option to improve interpersonal communications?
 a. Role-play everyday situations
 b. Read a dialogue and reproduce it using other words and expressions
 c. Listen to an audio recording and summarize it
 d. Write a letter or email to a friend

8. The most effective technique to expose students to different accents as a cultural aspect of the language is to:
 a. Read classic works from authors from different countries
 b. Listen to the instructor reading texts from authors from different countries
 c. Listen to TV commercials from different countries
 d. Make students read texts from different countries using different accents

9. When looking for the best way to improve writing skills, students should be asked to:
 a. Read a text and write a summary of it
 b. Listen to a text and answer a series of short written answers about it
 c. Read a text and answer a series of short written answers about it
 d. Write a text on a given topic

10. Select the best option to expand students' vocabulary about food.
 a. Give students a list of most common foods
 b. Make each student plan a meal and write the list of ingredients they need
 c. Role-play a dialogue between a customer and the cashier at a grocery store
 d. Role-play dialogues at a restaurant

11. Which of the following is the most effective suggestion for students that are trying to learn exceptions to gender rules for Spanish nouns?
 a. To make a list of all exceptions
 b. To learn them as they go
 c. To write every noun they learn with a definite article
 d. Not to worry as there are very few and unimportant exceptions

12. Which of the following is the most effective means to assess listening comprehension?

    a. Listen to a text and write a summary of it
    b. Listen to a text and write a dialogue about it
    c. Listen to a text and role-play the situation
    d. Listen to a text and answer a series of multiple choice questions about it

13. When looking for an interdisciplinary approach to teaching Spanish, which of the following would not be appropriate?

    a. Practice additions, subtractions, multiplications and divisions in Spanish
    b. Write a list of all irregular verbs in Spanish
    c. Talk in Spanish about the discovery of the New World
    d. Describe in Spanish paintings by Pablo Picasso

14. Which of the following options is not a good use of cooperative learning among students?

    a. To pair more advanced students with those with a lower level of Spanish on a joint project
    b. To assign a group project for researching the origins of cultural traditions
    c. To role-play everyday situations
    d. To ask each student to make a presentation in front of the rest of the class

15. Which of the following is the best tool to assess presentational skills?

    a. Read a summary of a given text
    b. Make an oral summary of a given text
    c. Ask questions about a given text
    d. Role-play a given dialogue

16. Which of the following internet uses helps the most to learn Spanish?

    a. Online chat room in Spanish
    b. Maps of Spanish-speaking countries from Google maps
    c. Menu from a tapas restaurant
    d. Website of the Prado museum

17. Watching a soap opera from Colombia is a good example of which of the following teaching techniques?

    a. Total physical response
    b. Lowering of affective filters
    c. Interdisciplinary instruction
    d. Technology-aided instruction

18. Which of the following would best indicate a strong cultural understanding?

    a. Knowing when to use *tú, vos* and *usted* when addressing a person
    b. Knowing when to use *el* and when to use *él*
    c. Knowing when to use *pedir* and when to use *preguntar*
    d. Knowing when to use *ser* and when to use *estar*

19. Which of the following is a good example of task-based teaching?

    a. Role playing a visit to the dentist's office
    b. Reading in Spanish a novel by Tom Clancy
    c. Writing a list of irregular verbs ending in *ar*
    d. Listening to a text and answering a series of questions

20. An instructor reads a series *of* instructions that the students must follow. This is <u>not</u> a good exercise to practice:

    a. Listening skills
    b. Comprehension skills
    c. (Interpretive skills)
    d. Interpersonal skills

Section 6 – Language Structures

1. Estamos planeando nuestras vacaciones. ¿Cuál es la expresión más adecuada?

    a. Fuimos de vacaciones a España.
    b. Vamos a ir de vacaciones a España.
    c. Estamos de vacaciones en España.
    d. Hemos ido de vacaciones a España.

2. Seleccione el adjetivo posesivo que mejor completa la frase siguiente:

Nosotros debemos terminar _____ informes antes de fin de mes.

    a. nuestras
    b. nuestros
    c. nuestra
    d. nuestro

3. ¿Cuál de las opciones a continuación se aplica mejor a la siguiente frase?

El ingeniero que vive <u>al lado de</u> mi casa es más joven que yo.

    engineer
    a. Yo soy viejo. —*old*
    b. El ingeniero de al lado de mi casa es joven. *young*
    c. Al lado de mi casa vive una persona más joven que yo.
    d. Mi casa es más vieja que la casa de al lado.

4. Quiero invitar a mis hermanos a cenar a mi casa. ¿Cuál es la expresión correcta?

    a. ¿Queremos venir a cenar a mi casa el viernes?
    b. ¿Quieres venir a cenar a mi casa el viernes?
    c. ¿Quiere venir a cenar a mi casa el viernes?
    d. ¿Quieren venir a mi casa el viernes?

5. ¿Cuál es la opción más apropiada para combinar las dos oraciones siguientes?

La maestra de español nos da tarea. La tarea es muy difícil.

    a. La tarea de español que nos da la maestra es muy difícil.
    b. La tarea que nos da la maestra de español es muy difícil.
    c. La maestra de español que nos da la tarea es muy difícil.
    d. Es difícil que la maestra de español nos dé tarea.

6. ¿Cuál es la opción que mejor completa la siguiente frase?

Vamos a ducharnos una vez que _____ el partido de tenis.

once

    a. terminaremos
    b. hayamos terminado
    c. terminábamos
    d. habíamos terminado

7. Escoja la opción que equivale a la siguiente frase:

Éste es mi libro, no tu libro.

    a. Este libro es mío, no tuyo.
    b. Este libro es a mí, no a ti.
    c. Este libro es de mí, no de ti.
    d. Este libro es de mío, no de tuyo.

8. ¿Qué expresión debo utilizar para preguntar el precio de un par de zapatos?

    a. ¿Cuánto cuesta los zapatos?
    b. ¿Cuántos cuestan los zapatos?
    c. ¿Cuánto cuestan los zapatos?
    d. ¿Cuántos cuesta los zapatos?

9. Completar la siguiente frase con la opción correcta.

El día tiene _____ horas.

    a. veinte y cuatro
    b. veinti y cuatro
    c. veinticuarto
    d. veinticuatro

10. Elija la opción correcta para completar la siguiente frase:

Pablo y Juan fueron compañeros de trabajo y _____ muy bien.

conocer – know/meet
saber – to know
to taste

    a. conocen
    b. se conocen
    c. saben
    d. se saben

For the questions 11-20, decide first whether the statement is correct or incorrect, then select the appropriate grammatical rule or explanation.

11. Los niños jugaban en el parque cuando empezó a llover

a. Incorrect	The Imperfect tense is used to denote a sudden action in the past
b. Incorrect	The Preterit tense is used to denote an ongoing action in the past
c. Correct	The Imperfect tense is used to denote an ongoing action in the past
d. Correct	The Preterit tense is used at least once in all sentences in the past.

12. Este es el libro de María.
    a. Incorrect   If used as the subject of a sentence *este* is written with an accent
    b. Incorrect   *Este* is always followed by a masculine, singular noun.
    c. Correct   If used as the subject of a sentence *este* does not have an accent
    d. Correct   *Este* is always followed by a conjugated verb.

13. La casa de el capitán está en la colina
    a. Incorrect   Capitán is feminine
    b. Incorrect   *De* + *el* are contracted into the one word *del*
    c. Correct   All definite articles agree in gender and number with the nouns they modify
    d. Correct   The verb agrees with the subject of the sentence

14. Carla es alta.
    a. Incorrect   *Estar* is used for permanent conditions
    b. Incorrect   *Estar* is used for temporary conditions
    c. Correct   *Ser* is used for permanent conditions
    d. Correct   *Ser* is used for temporary conditions

15. Siempre me ducho después de jugar al tenis.
    a. Incorrect   *Después* is always followed by the preposition *a*
    b. Incorrect   *Después* is never followed by a preposition
    c. Correct   *Después* sometimes requires to be followed by a preposition
    d. Correct   *Después* is always followed by the preposition *de*

16. El alumno preguntó permiso a la maestra para salir de la clase.
    a. Incorrect   The verb *pedir* is used to ask permission
    b. Incorrect   Neither *pedir* or *preguntar* can be used to ask permission
    c. Correct   The verb *preguntar* is used to ask permission
    d. Correct   Either *pedir* or *preguntar* can be used to ask permission

17. La mucama puso en la heladera todos los productos que ella compraron en el mercado.
    a. Incorrect   The pronoun of the second clause must agree with the direct object of the
    first clause
    b. Incorrect   The verb in each clause must agree with the subject of the clause
    c. Correct   The verb of the second clause must agree with the direct object of the first
    clause
    d. Correct   The pronoun of the second clause must agree with the subject of the first
    clause

18. El auto de Pedro es el más mejor del pueblo.
    a. Incorrect   *el mejor* is the correct form of the superlative of the adjective *bueno*
    b. Incorrect   *el mejor* is always used to form the superlative form of an adjective
    c. Correct   *el más* is always used to form the superlative form of an adjective
    d. Correct   *el más* is the correct form of the superlative of the adjective *mejor*

- 108 -

19. Necesito un destornillador para armar el juguete.
     a. Incorrect   The right preposition is *por*
     b. Incorrect   Both *por* and *para* are the wrong prepositions for this case
     c. Correct   I can use either *por* or *para*
     d. Correct   *Para* is the correct preposition

20. En el parque hay muchas niñas jugando.
     a. Incorrect   *Hay* should be in plural
     b. Incorrect   *Hay* should be in feminine
     c. Correct   *Hay* is the correct form for both plural and singular
     d. Correct   *Hay* is the correct form for plural

Answer Key and Explanations

Answers for Text #1

1. C: A "zoco" is a traditional market from the Arab countries of North Africa, brought to Spain by the Moors. The end of the second paragraph mentions the Moors and the traditional customs of these markets. Answer (a) is incorrect because El Rastro is located in an old Jewish neighborhood but is not a traditional Jewish flea market. Answer (b) is incorrect because it is never mentioned in the text that those selling at the market are from small communities from Madrid. Answer (d) is incorrect because the text mentions local craftsmen selling their products at the market live in the area but are not necessarily from it.

2. C: The first paragraph states that El Rastro was created in 1740, a year that belongs to the 18th century. Answer (a) is incorrect because the 17th century refers to the 1600s. The text never mentions who created El Rastro, therefore answers (b) and (d) are incorrect.

3. A: The second paragraph mentions antique items and objects. Answer (b) is incorrect because the last paragraph states that municipal regulations forbid the sale of food. Answer (c) is incorrect because the text does not mention imported crafts; the second paragraph mentions local crafts. Since answers (b) and (c) are incorrect, answer (d) is incorrect.

4. B: The last paragraph states that El Rastro is open Sundays and holidays in the morning until after lunch. Answer (a) is incorrect because it implies every morning, weekdays, weekends and holidays included. Answer (c) is incorrect because it indicates it is open Sundays and holidays only in the mornings. Answer (d) is incorrect because it suggests it is open only on holidays.

5. C: The meaning of "regatear" is to haggle or to barter, and refers to the negotiation of the price of an item and usually takes place in this kind of market. Answer (a) is incorrect because a reduction of the price may be a consequence of haggling but it is not the act itself. Answer (b) is incorrect because confirmation of the price may be a consequence of haggling but it is not the act itself. Answer (d) is incorrect because currency exchange may be part of haggling but it is not the act itself.

6. B: The second sentence of the last paragraph refers to the local people from Madrid that visits the market. Answer (a) is incorrect because the last paragraph talks about those visiting El Rastro, and not about those selling their products at the market. Answer (c) is incorrect because in the sentence the subject is the people who are used to do something and not the habit itself. Answer (d) is incorrect because food items cannot visit a market.

Answers for Text #2

1 B: The first sentence states Parra was born in a town south of Santiago, the capital of Chile. Since Santiago is in Chile, answers (a), (c) and (d) are incorrect.

2. D: In the middle of the first paragraph, it is stated that "her first marriage did not last long". Therefore she was married at least twice, making answers (a) and (b) incorrect. The text does not make any other reference to her marriages, consequently we do not know if she was married two or more times.

3. B: According to the text, in her song, Parra is thankful for her voice, her heart, laughing and crying, which allow her to express her feelings. Answer (a) is incorrect because the text does not

- 110 -

mention being alive as one of the things Parra is thankful. Answer (c) is incorrect because just two senses (sight and hearing) are mentioned. Answer (d) is incorrect because the text does not mention the love one as one of the things Parra is thankful.

4. C: Parra committed suicide taking her own life with a gunshot to her head. Answer (a) is incorrect because she did not die of a broken heart. Answer (b) is incorrect because the gunshot was not an accident. Answer (d) is incorrect because she did not have any tumor in her head.

5. D: Subjectivity in literary and musical expression is the definition of lyricism. Answer (a) is incorrect as the union of the soul with God is part of the definition of mysticism. Answers (b) and (c) are incorrect because they belong to the definition of classicism.

6. C: in the first paragraph, facts are presented chronologically. Answers (a) and (b) are incorrect because the ideas of the first paragraph are not in order of importance. Answer (d) is incorrect because the ideas of the first paragraph have a certain order.

Answers for Text #3

1. D: The first sentence of the text says oil is formed from terrestrial, marine, and lacustrine microorganisms.

2. D: The text states oil is stored in the pores of the reservoir. Answer (a) is incorrect because the source rock is where the oil is generated. Answer (b) is incorrect because the sealing layers are impermeable therefore cannot store oil. Answer (c) is incorrect because oil is stored at different depths below the surface of the Earth.

3. A: Oil subjected to higher temperatures over time converts to gas. Answer (b) is incorrect because you need time to generate oil and then more time to convert it to gas. Answer (c) is incorrect because higher temperatures are needed to break the long hydrocarbon chains of oil into the short ones of gas. Answer (d) is incorrect because lower temperatures do not break the oil's long chains and time is needed to achieve this breakage.

4. C: Geologists use seismic to study the distribution and characteristics of the rocks under the surface. Answer (a) is incorrect because the text states seismic is used to find <u>probable</u> places where oil <u>may</u> exist. Answer (b) is incorrect because seismic studies do not produce earthquakes. Answer (d) is incorrect because seismic surveys are done to select where to drill a well therefore they are run before drilling a well and not inside it.

5. A: One of the functions of the drilling mud is to cool the drilling bit. Answer (b) is incorrect because it is a function of the casing to prevent the collapse of the walls of the well. Answer (c) is incorrect because it is a function of the casing to isolate the different rock layers from each other. Answer (d) is incorrect because the drilling bit is the element that deepens the well.

6. B: The text describes how oil is formed and brought to the surface. Answer (a) is incorrect because the text does not narrate a story. Answer (c) is incorrect because the text is not a discussion of pros and cons. Answer (d) is incorrect because the text does not analyze the causes and effects of an event.

Answers for Text #4

1. C: The first sentence states that the plant can be found growing on its own, not purposely cultivated. Answer (a) is incorrect because the text does not say the plant grows unrestrained.

Answer (b) is incorrect because the text does not say the plant grows without limits. Answer (d) is incorrect because the text does not say the plant grows irresponsibly.

2. C: The loofah sponge is good for exfoliating the skin, a process that removes superficial dead cells. Answer (a) is incorrect because the text does not mention losing weight anywhere. Answer (b) is incorrect because the text does not say using a loofah sponge will eliminate wrinkles. Answer (d) is incorrect because the fruit of the loofah is soaked to remove its skin; a loofah sponge is not use to soak a person's skin.

3. B: To make bath products the loofah is first washed to remove the skin and seeds and then dried in the sun. Answer (a) is incorrect because the loofah is not only washed but also dried in the sun. Answer (c) is incorrect because the loofah is not ironed to make bath products; the text says it is ironed to make curtains, rugs and decorations. Answer (d) is incorrect for the same reasons answer c) is incorrect.

4. D: The first paragraph says that the Taller de la Lufa is a local cooperative. Answer (a) is incorrect; the Taller de la Lufa is not a private company. Answer (b) is incorrect; the Taller de la Lufa is not a public company. Answer (c) is incorrect; the Taller de la Lufa is not a state entity.

5. C: The farmers take their product to other places to get a better price. Answer (a) is incorrect because the Taller de la Lufa buys the farmers' crop. Answer (b) is incorrect because the Taller de la Lufa pays the farmers a just price. Answer (d) is incorrect because it does not say the farmers do not get along well with the Taller.

6. A: Students live and study at the center. Answer (b) is incorrect because the center is not a school in a residential neighborhood. Answer(c) is incorrect because the center is not a place to educate people who live in a residential neighborhood. Answer (d) is incorrect because the center is not just for students that do not live in it.

Answers for Text #5

1. C: The article was published in Le Cahier in Paris, France. Answer (a) is incorrect; the article is about a Mexican artistic development but was not published in Mexico. Answer (b) is incorrect, Carpentier was born in Cuba. Answer (d) is incorrect; the article mentions the USA ambassador but the article was not published in the USA.

2. D: According to the article, Rivera's personality was vigorous, complicated and variable. Answer (a) is incorrect; Rivera's personality was vigorous not weak. Answer (b) is incorrect; Rivera's personality was complicated not simple. Answer (c) is incorrect; Rivera's personality was variable not stable.

3. B: Rivera is considered to be responsible for the renaissance of the murals in Mexico. Answer (a) is incorrect; Rivera is responsible just for the renaissance of the murals in particular, not of all plastic art in general. Answer (c) is incorrect; Rivera just liked attitudes that ridicule. Answer (d) is incorrect; Rivera was not responsible for a renaissance of social painting.

4. D: Rivera was working on a fresco in the Palacio de Gobierno del Estado de Morelos in the city of Cuernavaca. The fresco was a gift of the American ambassador.

5. B: Rivera liked mocking images. Answer (a) is incorrect; Rivera liked caricatures and images that ridicule, not serious ones. Answer (c) is incorrect; Rivera liked aggressive, not placid attitudes.

Answer (d) is incorrect; Rivera painted big heads but the text does not specifically say he liked them.

6. A: The text emphasizes the importance of Rivera's frescos in the renaissance of this type of art in Mexico. Answer (b) is incorrect; Rivera's frescos are big and the text considers them very important. Answer (c) is incorrect; the text considers Rivera's frescos very important. Answer (d) is incorrect; the text does not say Rivera's frescos are colorful and charming.

Answers for Text #6

1. A: The first paragraph says some women see the financial responsibilities as an extra added to their list of things to do. Answer (b) is incorrect; taking care of financial responsibilities is not an obligation. Answer (c) is incorrect; the text does not say that taking care of financial responsibilities is a right women have. Answer (d) is incorrect; the text does not say that taking care of financial responsibilities is an option women have.

2. B: The text states that women should know about and have control over their financial situation. Answer (a) is incorrect; women are allowed to hire a consultant to help them with their finances. Answer (c) is incorrect; there are no laws forcing women to take care of their finances. Answer (d) is incorrect; women do not take care of their finances because they do not have anything better to do.

3. C: The second paragraph includes how much to save as one of the basic question every woman should know how to answer. Answer (a) is incorrect; the text does not say how to save. Answer (b) is incorrect; the third paragraph includes a question about saving for kids' college but it is not one of the basic questions a woman should know how to answer. Answer (d) is incorrect; the text does not say why to save.

4. C: The amount and variety of financial options are overwhelming. Answer (a) is incorrect; quantity and variety are not very limited. Answer (b) is incorrect; financial options are not known only by consultants. Answer (d) is incorrect; women have access to financial options.

5. D: Financial consultants can help invest money, analyze financial objectives, <u>and</u> assess financial situations.

6. C: The last two paragraphs clearly advertise the services of a financial firm. The first four paragraphs establish the basis for the advertisement. Answer (a) is incorrect; the text does not inform women about their financial rights. Answer (b) is incorrect; the text does not say women are financially incapable; on the contrary, it encourages women to take care of their finances. Answer (d) is incorrect; the text is not trying to recruit women to work for financial firms.

Answer for Visual #1

A: Incorrect. Fernando de Magallanes died in the Philippine Islands and never returned to Spain from his circumnavigation of the Earth. The first natives brought from America were presented to the King of Spain by Cristóbal Colón. The painting does not show any natives.

B: Incorrect. Galileo Galilei defended his heliocentric theory in a book and was later tried by the Holy Office or Roman Inquisition and forced to recant.

C: Incorrect. Queen Sofía and King Juan Carlos are the current monarchs of Spain. Hernán Cortés died in 1547.

D: Correct. Cristóbal Colón asked Isabel and Fernando for financial support to find a route to the East Indies by sailing west.

Answer for Visual #2

A: Correct. The ruins are high in the mountains and have the typical terraces and regularly shaped buildings of the Incas.

B: Incorrect. Teotihuacán is a pre-Colombian city in Mexico.

C: Incorrect. The Patagones, included in the broader category of the Teheulches, was a group of natives that lived in the South of Argentina and never reached Bolivia.

D: Incorrect. The Spanish conquistadores never built any temples to be used to worship Native American gods.

Answer for Visual #3

A: Incorrect. The word "jineteada" means "rodeo". The picture does not show any horses. We cannot infer the characters in the picture have been training any.

B: Correct. The title of the painting indicates it depicts a stop on the road. A small building, the "posta" is seen in the background. There is also a stagecoach to its right.

C: Incorrect. As mentioned in answer a), the picture does not show any horses and we cannot infer the characters in the picture have been training any.

D: Incorrect. The picture does not show any cattle. We cannot infer the characters in the picture have been herding any.

Answers for Curriculum/Instruction

1. D: To show difference and similarities between languages is a very effective way to introduce and reinforce grammar structures.

2. A: By being totally immersed in Spanish and with no English spoken, students learn Spanish by practicing their interpretation skills.

3. C: Authentic videos show cultural differences such as accent, words and expressions commonly used among Spanish-speaking countries.

4. D: By having to pay attention to describe their own clothes, students interact among themselves and with the teacher, and take an active part in expanding their vocabulary.

5. C: Multiple choice questions are a very good tool to evaluate specific grammar points. Since they do not involve any writing or conversation, they are very poor tools to evaluate writing, interpersonal and intercommunication skills.

6. B: Live recordings of formal and informal situations are very good tools to introduce the concept of *tú, vos* and *usted*. The other three options are techniques appropriate to explain and practice that concept.

7. A: By role-playing everyday situations students interact orally among them, improving interpersonal communications in the acquired language.

8. C: Accent is an oral aspect of the language and is best grasped by listening to authentic recordings (TV commercials, shows, films, etc.) from different countries.

9. D: Although the other three options are good writing practice, writing a complete text on a certain topic on their own makes students practice all aspects of writing (spelling, grammar, vocabulary, organization, etc.) without help from a given text.

10. B: The variety of options that will come up when each student plans a meal and writes the ingredients will expand the vocabulary of the group considerably better than the other, more vocabulary-restricted options.

11. C: Writing each noun with a definite article that shows its gender will point out whether it is an exception or not, and will help remember the correct gender.

12. D: Multiple choice questions asking particular aspects of the text and requiring specific answers are the best option to assess listening comprehension.

13. B: Writing a list of irregular verbs is part of the language itself and does not involve any other discipline.

14. D: A presentation does not involve any cooperation or work together among students.

15. B: An aural summary is basically a presentation of the text.

16. A: A chat room in Spanish is the most helpful as it requires students to practice comprehension as well as writing skills in Spanish.

17. D: Technologies such as audio and video recordings, combined with the power of computers and the internet, can be used to easily bring the culture being studied into the classroom.

18. A: The use of the different formal and informal ways of the second person singular is cultural and depends on the country. The other options refer to aspects of the language that apply to Spanish regardless of the country.

19. A: Task-based learning involves asking student to perform a meaningful task, such as going to the doctor, applying for a job, etc. in the acquired language.

20. D: There are no interpersonal skills involved in following instructions.

Answers for Language Structures

1. B: We are planning a vacation, which implies a future action. The structure *ir a* + infinitive denotes future.

2. B: The possessive adjective must agree in gender and number with the noun it modifies; *informes* is masculine, plural, therefore *nuestros* is the correct option.

3. C: The original sentence makes a comparison between the age of my neighbor and my age, not the houses. It does not say either that I am old or that the engineer is young, just that he is younger than I.

4. D: The verb must agree with the person(s) I am addressing, in this case, *my siblings*, second person plural (*ustedes quieren*).

5. B: In the original sentences, the adjective *español* modifies the noun *maestra*, and the adjective *difícil* modifies the noun *tarea*. Those relationships must be maintained in the combined sentence.

6. B: The expression *una vez que* requires the use of the subjunctive mode.

7. A: The long form of the possessive adjective is the correct way to replace the short form of the possessive adjective + a noun, and does not require a preposition.

8. C: *Cuánto* is used for singular (*how much*) and plural *(how many)*. The verb, though, must agree in number with the noun it refers to.

9. D: For cardinal numbers starting with *veinte*, the *e* changes to *i* and both digits are contracted into one single word.

10. B: The verb *conocer* is used to express knowing a person; in this case, it must be used in the reflexive mode to show it is a two-way relationship and they know each other.

11. C: The Imperfect tense is used to denote an ongoing action in the past *(jugaban),* and the Preterit tense is used to denote a sudden action in the past (*empezó*). The Preterit tense is not necessarily used at least once in all sentences in the past.

12. A: The demonstrative pronoun *éste*, with a written accent, is the correct stand-alone option as the subject of a sentence. The demonstrative adjective *este*, without a written accent, is always followed by a masculine, singular noun.

13. B: When followed by the definite article *el*, prepositions *de* and *a* have the contracted form *del* and *al*, respectively.

14. C: Height is a permanent condition in a person; therefore *ser* is the correct verb to use.

15. D: The preposition *de* always goes after *después*, regardless of the type of structure that follows (verb, noun, etc.)

16. A: The verb *to ask* has to different translation: *pedir* when it is a request and *preguntar* when it is a question. In this case the student is requesting permission therefore *pedir* should be used.

17. B: Verbs must always agree with the subject that performs the action, in this case it should be *ella compró*.

18. A: Although in the majority of the cases *el más + adjective* is used to form the superlative form of adjectives, there are a few exceptions, among them the adjective *bueno* whose superlative is *el mejor*.

19. D: *Para* is the correct preposition to denote purpose.

20. C: *Hay* is the correct form for both singular (there is) and plural (there are) nouns.

How to Overcome Test Anxiety

Just the thought of taking a test is enough to make most people a little nervous. A test is an important event that can have a long-term impact on your future, so it's important to take it seriously and it's natural to feel anxious about performing well. But just because anxiety is normal, that doesn't mean that it's helpful in test taking, or that you should simply accept it as part of your life. Anxiety can have a variety of effects. These effects can be mild, like making you feel slightly nervous, or severe, like blocking your ability to focus or remember even a simple detail.

If you experience test anxiety—whether severe or mild—it's important to know how to beat it. To discover this, first you need to understand what causes test anxiety.

Causes of Test Anxiety

While we often think of anxiety as an uncontrollable emotional state, it can actually be caused by simple, practical things. One of the most common causes of test anxiety is that a person does not feel adequately prepared for their test. This feeling can be the result of many different issues such as poor study habits or lack of organization, but the most common culprit is time management. Starting to study too late, failing to organize your study time to cover all of the material, or being distracted while you study will mean that you're not well prepared for the test. This may lead to cramming the night before, which will cause you to be physically and mentally exhausted for the test. Poor time management also contributes to feelings of stress, fear, and hopelessness as you realize you are not well prepared but don't know what to do about it.

Other times, test anxiety is not related to your preparation for the test but comes from unresolved fear. This may be a past failure on a test, or poor performance on tests in general. It may come from comparing yourself to others who seem to be performing better or from the stress of living up to expectations. Anxiety may be driven by fears of the future—how failure on this test would affect your educational and career goals. These fears are often completely irrational, but they can still negatively impact your test performance.

> **Review Video:** 3 Reasons You Have Test Anxiety
> Visit mometrix.com/academy and enter code: 428468

Elements of Test Anxiety

As mentioned earlier, test anxiety is considered to be an emotional state, but it has physical and mental components as well. Sometimes you may not even realize that you are suffering from test anxiety until you notice the physical symptoms. These can include trembling hands, rapid heartbeat, sweating, nausea, and tense muscles. Extreme anxiety may lead to fainting or vomiting. Obviously, any of these symptoms can have a negative impact on testing. It is important to recognize them as soon as they begin to occur so that you can address the problem before it damages your performance.

> **Review Video:** 3 Ways to Tell You Have Test Anxiety
> Visit mometrix.com/academy and enter code: 927847

The mental components of test anxiety include trouble focusing and inability to remember learned information. During a test, your mind is on high alert, which can help you recall information and stay focused for an extended period of time. However, anxiety interferes with your mind's natural processes, causing you to blank out, even on the questions you know well. The strain of testing during anxiety makes it difficult to stay focused, especially on a test that may take several hours. Extreme anxiety can take a huge mental toll, making it difficult not only to recall test information but even to understand the test questions or pull your thoughts together.

> **Review Video:** How Test Anxiety Affects Memory
> Visit mometrix.com/academy and enter code: 609003

Effects of Test Anxiety

Test anxiety is like a disease—if left untreated, it will get progressively worse. Anxiety leads to poor performance, and this reinforces the feelings of fear and failure, which in turn lead to poor performances on subsequent tests. It can grow from a mild nervousness to a crippling condition. If allowed to progress, test anxiety can have a big impact on your schooling, and consequently on your future.

Test anxiety can spread to other parts of your life. Anxiety on tests can become anxiety in any stressful situation, and blanking on a test can turn into panicking in a job situation. But fortunately, you don't have to let anxiety rule your testing and determine your grades. There are a number of relatively simple steps you can take to move past anxiety and function normally on a test and in the rest of life.

> **Review Video:** How Test Anxiety Impacts Your Grades
> Visit mometrix.com/academy and enter code: 939819

Physical Steps for Beating Test Anxiety

While test anxiety is a serious problem, the good news is that it can be overcome. It doesn't have to control your ability to think and remember information. While it may take time, you can begin taking steps today to beat anxiety.

Just as your first hint that you may be struggling with anxiety comes from the physical symptoms, the first step to treating it is also physical. Rest is crucial for having a clear, strong mind. If you are tired, it is much easier to give in to anxiety. But if you establish good sleep habits, your body and mind will be ready to perform optimally, without the strain of exhaustion. Additionally, sleeping well helps you to retain information better, so you're more likely to recall the answers when you see the test questions.

Getting good sleep means more than going to bed on time. It's important to allow your brain time to relax. Take study breaks from time to time so it doesn't get overworked, and don't study right before bed. Take time to rest your mind before trying to rest your body, or you may find it difficult to fall asleep.

> **Review Video: The Importance of Sleep for Your Brain**
> Visit mometrix.com/academy and enter code: 319338

Along with sleep, other aspects of physical health are important in preparing for a test. Good nutrition is vital for good brain function. Sugary foods and drinks may give a burst of energy but this burst is followed by a crash, both physically and emotionally. Instead, fuel your body with protein and vitamin-rich foods.

Also, drink plenty of water. Dehydration can lead to headaches and exhaustion, especially if your brain is already under stress from the rigors of the test. Particularly if your test is a long one, drink water during the breaks. And if possible, take an energy-boosting snack to eat between sections.

> **Review Video: How Diet Can Affect your Mood**
> Visit mometrix.com/academy and enter code: 624317

Along with sleep and diet, a third important part of physical health is exercise. Maintaining a steady workout schedule is helpful, but even taking 5-minute study breaks to walk can help get your blood pumping faster and clear your head. Exercise also releases endorphins, which contribute to a positive feeling and can help combat test anxiety.

When you nurture your physical health, you are also contributing to your mental health. If your body is healthy, your mind is much more likely to be healthy as well. So take time to rest, nourish your body with healthy food and water, and get moving as much as possible. Taking these physical steps will make you stronger and more able to take the mental steps necessary to overcome test anxiety.

> **Review Video: How to Stay Healthy and Prevent Test Anxiety**
> Visit mometrix.com/academy and enter code: 877894

Mental Steps for Beating Test Anxiety

Working on the mental side of test anxiety can be more challenging, but as with the physical side, there are clear steps you can take to overcome it. As mentioned earlier, test anxiety often stems from lack of preparation, so the obvious solution is to prepare for the test. Effective studying may be the most important weapon you have for beating test anxiety, but you can and should employ several other mental tools to combat fear.

First, boost your confidence by reminding yourself of past success—tests or projects that you aced. If you're putting as much effort into preparing for this test as you did for those, there's no reason you should expect to fail here. Work hard to prepare; then trust your preparation.

Second, surround yourself with encouraging people. It can be helpful to find a study group, but be sure that the people you're around will encourage a positive attitude. If you spend time with others who are anxious or cynical, this will only contribute to your own anxiety. Look for others who are motivated to study hard from a desire to succeed, not from a fear of failure.

Third, reward yourself. A test is physically and mentally tiring, even without anxiety, and it can be helpful to have something to look forward to. Plan an activity following the test, regardless of the outcome, such as going to a movie or getting ice cream.

When you are taking the test, if you find yourself beginning to feel anxious, remind yourself that you know the material. Visualize successfully completing the test. Then take a few deep, relaxing breaths and return to it. Work through the questions carefully but with confidence, knowing that you are capable of succeeding.

Developing a healthy mental approach to test taking will also aid in other areas of life. Test anxiety affects more than just the actual test—it can be damaging to your mental health and even contribute to depression. It's important to beat test anxiety before it becomes a problem for more than testing.

> **Review Video: Test Anxiety and Depression**
> Visit mometrix.com/academy and enter code: 904704

Study Strategy

Being prepared for the test is necessary to combat anxiety, but what does being prepared look like? You may study for hours on end and still not feel prepared. What you need is a strategy for test prep. The next few pages outline our recommended steps to help you plan out and conquer the challenge of preparation.

Step 1: Scope Out the Test

Learn everything you can about the format (multiple choice, essay, etc.) and what will be on the test. Gather any study materials, course outlines, or sample exams that may be available. Not only will this help you to prepare, but knowing what to expect can help to alleviate test anxiety.

Step 2: Map Out the Material

Look through the textbook or study guide and make note of how many chapters or sections it has. Then divide these over the time you have. For example, if a book has 15 chapters and you have five days to study, you need to cover three chapters each day. Even better, if you have the time, leave an extra day at the end for overall review after you have gone through the material in depth.

If time is limited, you may need to prioritize the material. Look through it and make note of which sections you think you already have a good grasp on, and which need review. While you are studying, skim quickly through the familiar sections and take more time on the challenging parts. Write out your plan so you don't get lost as you go. Having a written plan also helps you feel more in control of the study, so anxiety is less likely to arise from feeling overwhelmed at the amount to cover. A sample plan may look like this:

- Day 1: Skim chapters 1–4, study chapter 5 (especially pages 31–33)
- Day 2: Study chapters 6–7, skim chapters 8–9
- Day 3: Skim chapter 10, study chapters 11–12 (especially pages 87–90)
- Day 4: Study chapters 13–15
- Day 5: Overall review (focus most on chapters 5, 6, and 12), take practice test

Step 3: Gather Your Tools

Decide what study method works best for you. Do you prefer to highlight in the book as you study and then go back over the highlighted portions? Or do you type out notes of the important information? Or is it helpful to make flashcards that you can carry with you? Assemble the pens, index cards, highlighters, post-it notes, and any other materials you may need so you won't be distracted by getting up to find things while you study.

If you're having a hard time retaining the information or organizing your notes, experiment with different methods. For example, try color-coding by subject with colored pens, highlighters, or post-it notes. If you learn better by hearing, try recording yourself reading your notes so you can listen while in the car, working out, or simply sitting at your desk. Ask a friend to quiz you from your flashcards, or try teaching someone the material to solidify it in your mind.

Step 4: Create Your Environment

It's important to avoid distractions while you study. This includes both the obvious distractions like visitors and the subtle distractions like an uncomfortable chair (or a too-comfortable couch that makes you want to fall asleep). Set up the best study environment possible: good lighting and a comfortable work area. If background music helps you focus, you may want to turn it on, but otherwise keep the room quiet. If you are using a computer to take notes, be sure you don't have any other windows open, especially applications like social media, games, or anything else that could distract you. Silence your phone and turn off notifications. Be sure to keep water close by so you stay hydrated while you study (but avoid unhealthy drinks and snacks).

Also, take into account the best time of day to study. Are you freshest first thing in the morning? Try to set aside some time then to work through the material. Is your mind clearer in the afternoon or evening? Schedule your study session then. Another method is to study at the same time of day that you will take the test, so that your brain gets used to working on the material at that time and will be ready to focus at test time.

Step 5: Study!

Once you have done all the study preparation, it's time to settle into the actual studying. Sit down, take a few moments to settle your mind so you can focus, and begin to follow your study plan. Don't give in to distractions or let yourself procrastinate. This is your time to prepare so you'll be ready to fearlessly approach the test. Make the most of the time and stay focused.

Of course, you don't want to burn out. If you study too long you may find that you're not retaining the information very well. Take regular study breaks. For example, taking five minutes out of every hour to walk briskly, breathing deeply and swinging your arms, can help your mind stay fresh.

As you get to the end of each chapter or section, it's a good idea to do a quick review. Remind yourself of what you learned and work on any difficult parts. When you feel that you've mastered the material, move on to the next part. At the end of your study session, briefly skim through your notes again.

But while review is helpful, cramming last minute is NOT. If at all possible, work ahead so that you won't need to fit all your study into the last day. Cramming overloads your brain with more information than it can process and retain, and your tired mind may struggle to recall even previously learned information when it is overwhelmed with last-minute study. Also, the urgent nature of cramming and the stress placed on your brain contribute to anxiety. You'll be more likely to go to the test feeling unprepared and having trouble thinking clearly.

So don't cram, and don't stay up late before the test, even just to review your notes at a leisurely pace. Your brain needs rest more than it needs to go over the information again. In fact, plan to finish your studies by noon or early afternoon the day before the test. Give your brain the rest of the day to relax or focus on other things, and get a good night's sleep. Then you will be fresh for the test and better able to recall what you've studied.

Step 6: Take a practice test

Many courses offer sample tests, either online or in the study materials. This is an excellent resource to check whether you have mastered the material, as well as to prepare for the test format and environment.

Check the test format ahead of time: the number of questions, the type (multiple choice, free response, etc.), and the time limit. Then create a plan for working through them. For example, if you have 30 minutes to take a 60-question test, your limit is 30 seconds per question. Spend less time on the questions you know well so that you can take more time on the difficult ones.

If you have time to take several practice tests, take the first one open book, with no time limit. Work through the questions at your own pace and make sure you fully understand them. Gradually work up to taking a test under test conditions: sit at a desk with all study materials put away and set a timer. Pace yourself to make sure you finish the test with time to spare and go back to check your answers if you have time.

After each test, check your answers. On the questions you missed, be sure you understand why you missed them. Did you misread the question (tests can use tricky wording)? Did you forget the information? Or was it something you hadn't learned? Go back and study any shaky areas that the practice tests reveal.

Taking these tests not only helps with your grade, but also aids in combating test anxiety. If you're already used to the test conditions, you're less likely to worry about it, and working through tests until you're scoring well gives you a confidence boost. Go through the practice tests until you feel comfortable, and then you can go into the test knowing that you're ready for it.

Test Tips

On test day, you should be confident, knowing that you've prepared well and are ready to answer the questions. But aside from preparation, there are several test day strategies you can employ to maximize your performance.

First, as stated before, get a good night's sleep the night before the test (and for several nights before that, if possible). Go into the test with a fresh, alert mind rather than staying up late to study.

Try not to change too much about your normal routine on the day of the test. It's important to eat a nutritious breakfast, but if you normally don't eat breakfast at all, consider eating just a protein bar. If you're a coffee drinker, go ahead and have your normal coffee. Just make sure you time it so that the caffeine doesn't wear off right in the middle of your test. Avoid sugary beverages, and drink enough water to stay hydrated but not so much that you need a restroom break 10 minutes into the test. If your test isn't first thing in the morning, consider going for a walk or doing a light workout before the test to get your blood flowing.

Allow yourself enough time to get ready, and leave for the test with plenty of time to spare so you won't have the anxiety of scrambling to arrive in time. Another reason to be early is to select a good seat. It's helpful to sit away from doors and windows, which can be distracting. Find a good seat, get out your supplies, and settle your mind before the test begins.

When the test begins, start by going over the instructions carefully, even if you already know what to expect. Make sure you avoid any careless mistakes by following the directions.

Then begin working through the questions, pacing yourself as you've practiced. If you're not sure on an answer, don't spend too much time on it, and don't let it shake your confidence. Either skip it and come back later, or eliminate as many wrong answers as possible and guess among the remaining ones. Don't dwell on these questions as you continue—put them out of your mind and focus on what lies ahead.

Be sure to read all of the answer choices, even if you're sure the first one is the right answer. Sometimes you'll find a better one if you keep reading. But don't second-guess yourself if you do immediately know the answer. Your gut instinct is usually right. Don't let test anxiety rob you of the information you know.

If you have time at the end of the test (and if the test format allows), go back and review your answers. Be cautious about changing any, since your first instinct tends to be correct, but make sure you didn't misread any of the questions or accidentally mark the wrong answer choice. Look over any you skipped and make an educated guess.

At the end, leave the test feeling confident. You've done your best, so don't waste time worrying about your performance or wishing you could change anything. Instead, celebrate the successful completion of this test. And finally, use this test to learn how to deal with anxiety even better next time.

> **Review Video: 5 Tips to Beat Test Anxiety**
> Visit mometrix.com/academy and enter code: 570656

Important Qualification

Not all anxiety is created equal. If your test anxiety is causing major issues in your life beyond the classroom or testing center, or if you are experiencing troubling physical symptoms related to your anxiety, it may be a sign of a serious physiological or psychological condition. If this sounds like your situation, we strongly encourage you to seek professional help.

Thank You

We at Mometrix would like to extend our heartfelt thanks to you, our friend and patron, for allowing us to play a part in your journey. It is a privilege to serve people from all walks of life who are unified in their commitment to building the best future they can for themselves.

The preparation you devote to these important testing milestones may be the most valuable educational opportunity you have for making a real difference in your life. We encourage you to put your heart into it—that feeling of succeeding, overcoming, and yes, conquering will be well worth the hours you've invested.

We want to hear your story, your struggles and your successes, and if you see any opportunities for us to improve our materials so we can help others even more effectively in the future, please share that with us as well. **The team at Mometrix would be absolutely thrilled to hear from you!** So please, send us an email (support@mometrix.com) and let's stay in touch.

If you'd like some additional help, check out these other resources we offer for your exam:

http://mometrixflashcards.com/MTTC

Additional Bonus Material

Due to our efforts to try to keep this book to a manageable length, we've created a link that will give you access to all of your additional bonus material.

Please visit https://www.mometrix.com/bonus948/mttcspanish to access the information.